Stats in a Snap: The Ultimate Guide to Official Statistics

K K MONI and S K CHOUDHARY

Published by K K MONI, 2025.

STATS IN A SNAP: THE ULTIMATE GUIDE TO OFFICIAL STATISTICS

First edition. January 31, 2025.

ISBN: 979-8230526407

Written by K K MONI and S K CHOUDHARY.

Table of Contents

Dedicated...

To my beloved Team of SUNRISE CLASSES,whose unwavering support, boundless love, and quiet strength have been my guiding light in every step of this journey.

To my students,who inspire me to dream bigger, work harder, and believe in the power of education to change lives.

And to my friends,for their encouragement, patience, and belief in me, even on the days when I doubted myself.

This book is for all of you, with immense gratitude and love.

— K K Moni & S K Choudhary

"Official statistics are the mirror of a nation's progress, reflecting the truths that guide decisions, shape policies, and empower societies to grow with purpose."

FOREWORD

Stats in a Snap: The Ultimate Guide to Official Statistics

In a world driven by data, understanding official statistics has never been more important. "**Stats in a Snap**" is a comprehensive guide that demystifies the intricate realm of official statistics, making it accessible to readers from all walks of life. Whether you are a policymaker shaping the future, a business leader seeking market insights, or a curious individual wanting to understand the numbers that govern our world, this book has something to offer.

What This Book Offers

1. **A Complete Introduction to Official Statistics** Learn how governments, businesses, and organizations rely on official statistics for evidence-based decision-making. Explore the historical development of statistical systems and their pivotal role in modern governance, economic planning, and social progress.
2. **National and International Perspectives** Gain insights into the structure and workings of statistical systems, from India's National Statistical Organization to global entities like the United Nations Statistical Commission. Understand how these bodies coordinate to produce reliable, comparable data across nations.
3. **Innovative Data Collection Methods** Dive into traditional techniques like surveys and censuses, and explore cutting-edge approaches involving big data, satellite imagery, and administrative records. Discover how these methods combine to create accurate, timely, and granular statistics.
4. **Quality Assurance and Reliability** Understand the rigorous

processes statistical agencies employ to ensure data accuracy, precision, and credibility. Learn how to assess and interpret statistical outputs with a critical eye, identifying potential biases and errors.

5. **Practical Applications Across Sectors** Explore the transformative impact of official statistics on economic planning, social policy, healthcare, education, and environmental monitoring. Real-world examples illustrate how data informs critical decisions and fosters development.
6. **Focus on India's Statistical System** For readers interested in one of the world's largest democracies, the book provides a deep dive into India's statistical landscape. From the Economic Census to the National Sample Surveys, uncover the methodologies and innovations driving India's data revolution.
7. **Global Challenges and Emerging Trends** Address the challenges posed by rapid technological changes, data privacy concerns, and the proliferation of misinformation. Learn how statistical systems are adapting to evolving needs and leveraging artificial intelligence, big data, and open data initiatives to stay ahead.

Who Should Read This Book?

- **Policymakers and Government Officials**: Build a strong foundation for evidence-based decision-making.

- **Business Professionals**: Gain insights into market trends, economic indicators, and demographic data for strategic planning.

- **Students and Academics**: Complement your studies with a solid understanding of official statistics and methodologies.
- **Journalists and Media Professionals**: Accurately interpret and report statistical data to inform the public.
- **General Readers**: Become a more informed citizen by understanding the data shaping public policies and global challenges.

Why This Book Stands Out

Unlike traditional textbooks, **"Stats in a Snap"** adopts a holistic and engaging approach, blending technical details with historical context, case studies, and real-world applications. It simplifies complex concepts, making them accessible to readers with little or no background in mathematics or statistics.

With a focus on practical skills, the book empowers readers to:

- Interpret and evaluate statistical claims critically.
- Communicate data insights effectively using visualization techniques.
- Stay informed about the latest trends in data-driven decision-making.

A Call to Action

Official statistics are not just numbers—they are tools that shape societies, measure progress, and address global challenges. **"Stats in a Snap"** invites you to embark on a journey through the fascinating world of data. By the end, you'll not only understand the numbers but also gain the confidence to engage with them meaningfully.

Get ready to see the world through a statistical lens. **The journey starts here.**

INTRODUCTION

Have you ever wondered how governments make crucial decisions that shape our lives? Or how businesses determine which products to launch in new markets? The answers often lie hidden within a realm of numbers, percentages, and intricate data sets known as official statistics. These powerful tools form the backbone of modern governance, economic planning, and social development. Yet, for many, the world of official statistics remains a mysterious and intimidating landscape. "Stats in a Snap: The Ultimate Guide to Official Statistics" is here to change that perception, offering readers a comprehensive and accessible journey through this essential field.

In an era where data drives decision-making at every level, understanding official statistics has never been more critical. From determining economic policies that affect millions to shaping healthcare initiatives that save lives, these numbers wield immense influence. However, the complexity and vastness of statistical systems often deter many from exploring this crucial domain. This book aims to demystify official statistics, presenting them in a format that is both engaging and easy to comprehend, regardless of your background in mathematics or economics.

What sets "Stats in a Snap" apart is its holistic approach to the subject. While many books focus solely on the technical aspects of statistics, this guide goes beyond, exploring the historical context, institutional frameworks, and real-world applications of official statistics. It offers readers not just the 'what' but also the 'why' and 'how' of statistical systems, providing a 360-degree view of this fascinating field.

The book covers several key themes that are crucial for anyone looking to understand the world of official statistics. First, it delves into the structure and organization of national and international statistical systems, offering insights into the complex machinery that produces the numbers we rely on daily. From the United Nations Statistical Commission to national bodies like India's National Statistical Organization, readers will gain a comprehensive understanding of the institutions that shape our statistical landscape.

Secondly, the book explores the various methodologies employed in data collection and dissemination. It sheds light on traditional methods like surveys and censuses, while also discussing emerging trends such as big data analytics and open data initiatives. This blend of old and new provides readers with a nuanced understanding of how official statistics are evolving in the digital age.

Another crucial theme is the reliability and quality of official statistics. In an era of 'fake news' and information overload, understanding how to assess the accuracy and precision of statistical data is more important than ever. The book offers valuable insights into quality assurance methods and ways to identify and address biases in statistical reporting.

Furthermore, "Stats in a Snap" provides an in-depth look at various types of statistics and their applications. From agricultural and industrial statistics to vital statistics and social indicators, the book covers a wide range of topics, demonstrating how these numbers impact every aspect of our lives. It also delves into complex concepts like index numbers and national accounts, breaking them down into digestible segments that even statistical novices can grasp.

Lastly, the book places a special focus on the Indian statistical system, making it particularly relevant for readers interested in understanding the statistical landscape of one of the world's largest democracies and fastest-growing economies. From the National Sample Survey to the Economic Census, it offers a comprehensive overview of India's major statistical activities and initiatives.

Who stands to benefit from this book? The answer is simple: everyone. Whether you're a policymaker looking to make more informed decisions, a business professional seeking to understand market trends, a student aspiring to enter the field of data science, or simply a curious citizen wanting to make sense of the numbers that shape our world, "Stats in a Snap" has something to offer you.

For policymakers and government officials, this book provides a robust framework for understanding and utilizing official statistics in decision-making processes. It offers insights into how different countries and international organizations structure their statistical systems, enabling readers to draw valuable lessons and best practices.

Business professionals will find the book invaluable in understanding economic indicators, market trends, and demographic data that can inform strategic decisions. The sections on industrial statistics, price indices, and national accounts are particularly relevant for those in the corporate world looking to gain a competitive edge through data-driven insights.

Students and academics in fields such as economics, sociology, public policy, and data science will discover a wealth of information that complements their studies. The book's comprehensive coverage of statistical methodologies, data collection techniques, and quality assurance measures provides a solid foundation for those looking to specialize in statistics or related fields.

Journalists and media professionals will find "Stats in a Snap" an essential resource for interpreting and reporting on official statistics accurately. In an age where data journalism is gaining prominence, understanding the nuances of statistical systems and their outputs is crucial for delivering informed and impactful stories.

Even for the general reader, this book offers a pathway to becoming a more informed citizen. In a world where numbers often drive public discourse and policy decisions, understanding official statistics empowers individuals to engage more meaningfully in civic discussions and make better-informed personal decisions.

By reading "Stats in a Snap," you'll gain much more than just a theoretical understanding of official statistics. You'll develop practical skills in interpreting statistical data, recognizing reliable sources of information, and applying statistical insights to real-world situations. The book's focus on data visualization techniques and dissemination strategies will enhance your ability to communicate complex statistical information effectively.

Moreover, you'll gain a deeper appreciation for the role of statistics in shaping our world. From tracking progress towards sustainable development goals to measuring gender equality and human development, official statistics play a crucial role in addressing some of the most pressing challenges of our time. This book will equip you with the knowledge to understand these global issues through a statistical lens.

You'll also develop a critical eye for evaluating statistical claims, a skill that is increasingly valuable in our data-driven world. The book's sections on reliability and quality assurance will teach you to question data sources, understand margins of error, and recognize potential biases in statistical reporting. This knowledge is invaluable in an era where statistics are often misused or misinterpreted in public discourse.

For those interested in career opportunities, "Stats in a Snap" opens up a world of possibilities. The field of official statistics offers diverse career paths, from data scientists and economists to policy analysts and international development professionals. This book provides a comprehensive overview of the field, helping readers identify areas of interest and potential career trajectories.

Furthermore, the book's focus on emerging trends in official statistics, such as big data analytics and open data initiatives, prepares readers for the future of the field. As statistical systems evolve to incorporate new technologies and methodologies, the insights provided in this book will help you stay ahead of the curve and adapt to changing data landscapes.

One of the unique aspects of "Stats in a Snap" is its global perspective combined with a specific focus on the Indian statistical system. This dual approach allows readers to understand universal principles of official statistics while also gaining insights into how these principles are applied in one of the world's most complex and diverse nations. For anyone interested in global development, emerging markets, or comparative statistical systems, this perspective is invaluable.

The book also addresses some of the most pressing challenges facing official statistics today. It explores how statistical systems are adapting to rapid technological changes, addressing issues of data privacy and security, and striving to provide timely and relevant information in an increasingly fast-paced world. By understanding these challenges, readers will be better equipped to contribute to discussions about the future of official statistics and data-driven decision-making.

"Stats in a Snap" doesn't just present dry facts and figures. It brings statistics to life through real-world examples, case studies, and historical anecdotes. You'll learn about the origins of modern statistical systems, the visionaries who shaped the field, and the pivotal moments that transformed how we collect and use data. These stories make the subject matter more relatable and memorable, helping you connect abstract concepts to tangible realities.

As you delve into the pages of this book, you'll discover that official statistics are not just numbers on a page or data points in a spreadsheet. They are powerful tools that can illuminate social issues, guide economic policies, and even save lives. From tracking the spread of diseases to measuring the impact of climate change, official statistics play a crucial role in addressing some of the most pressing challenges of our time.

You'll also gain a new appreciation for the complexity and rigor involved in producing official statistics. Behind every number is a carefully designed methodology, a team of dedicated professionals, and a commitment to accuracy and impartiality. Understanding this process will give you a new level of respect for the data we often take for granted and make you a more discerning consumer of statistical information.

Moreover, "Stats in a Snap" will empower you to be an active participant in the world of official statistics. You'll learn about open data initiatives and how citizens can access and use official statistics for their own research, advocacy, or personal interest. This knowledge opens up exciting possibilities for civic engagement and data-driven activism.

The book also touches on the ethical considerations in official statistics, including issues of data privacy, confidentiality, and the responsible use of statistical information. In an era where data is often referred to as the "new oil," understanding these ethical dimensions is crucial for anyone involved in collecting, analyzing, or disseminating statistical information.

As you progress through the chapters, you'll find that your perception of the world around you begins to shift. You'll start seeing patterns and trends where you once saw only random events. News reports will take on new meaning as you understand the statistical foundations behind the headlines. Policy debates will become clearer as you recognize the data driving different positions. In essence, "Stats in a Snap" doesn't just teach you about statistics; it gives you a new lens through which to view and understand the world.

But perhaps the most valuable takeaway from this book is the confidence it will instill in you to engage with statistical information. No longer will you feel intimidated by complex data sets or overwhelmed by statistical jargon. Instead, you'll have the tools and knowledge to approach official statistics with curiosity and critical thinking. Whether you're analyzing a government report, interpreting economic indicators, or simply trying to make sense of the latest poll results, you'll do so with a newfound sense of competence and insight.

As we stand on the brink of a new era in official statistics, where big data, artificial intelligence, and machine learning are reshaping traditional methodologies, the knowledge you gain from this book will be more valuable than ever. It will provide you with a solid foundation to understand these emerging trends and their implications for the future of data-driven decision-making.

In conclusion, "Stats in a Snap: The Ultimate Guide to Official Statistics" is more than just a book about numbers and data collection methods. It's a key that unlocks a deeper understanding of how our world operates, how decisions are made, and how progress is measured. It's an invitation to join a community of informed citizens who can critically engage with the statistical information that shapes our lives.

So, are you ready to embark on this enlightening journey through the world of official statistics? Are you prepared to transform the way you see data and its impact on society? Turn the page, and let's begin this exciting exploration together. The world of official statistics awaits, and with "Stats in a Snap" as your guide, you're about to discover just how fascinating, relevant, and accessible this field can be. Welcome to a new way of understanding our data-driven world – let's dive in!

Chapter 1: Introduction to Official Statistics

Official statistics form the backbone of informed decision-making in modern societies. They provide a quantitative foundation for understanding the complex social, economic, and environmental phenomena that shape our world. In this chapter, we will explore the definition and importance of official statistics, their crucial role in policy-making and governance, and the historical development of statistical systems that have led to the sophisticated data collection and analysis methods we rely on today.

Official statistics can be defined as numerical data produced by government agencies or other public bodies, following strict methodological and quality standards. These statistics are designed to provide an accurate and comprehensive picture of various aspects of a country's society, economy, and environment. They are characterized by their reliability, objectivity, and relevance to public policy and decision-making processes.

The importance of official statistics cannot be overstated. They serve as a mirror to society, reflecting its current state and trends, and enabling policymakers, researchers, and citizens to make informed decisions based on empirical evidence rather than assumptions or anecdotes. As the renowned statistician William Edwards Deming once said, "In God we trust; all others must bring data." This quote encapsulates the critical role that official statistics play in providing a factual basis for understanding and addressing societal challenges.

One of the primary functions of official statistics is to support evidence-based policy-making. Governments rely on these statistics to identify problems, set priorities, and evaluate the effectiveness of their policies and programs. For instance, unemployment rates guide labor market policies, while inflation figures inform monetary policy decisions. Population statistics are essential for planning public services, such as healthcare and education. Without accurate and timely official statistics, policymakers would be navigating in the dark, potentially leading to misallocation of resources and ineffective interventions.

Official statistics also play a crucial role in democratic governance by promoting transparency and accountability. By providing citizens with access to reliable information about their country's performance across various domains, official statistics empower the public to hold their governments accountable. This transparency fosters trust between citizens and their government, a cornerstone of a healthy democracy. As the United Nations Fundamental Principles of Official Statistics state, "Official statistics provide an indispensable element in the information system of a democratic society, serving the government, the economy and the public with data about the economic, demographic, social and environmental situation."

The use of statistics in governance is not a recent phenomenon. In fact, the word "statistics" itself is derived from the Latin "statisticum collegium" (state advisor) and the Italian "statista" (statesman or politician). The historical development of statistical systems can be traced back to ancient civilizations, where rudimentary forms of data collection were used for taxation and military purposes. However, the modern concept of official statistics as we know it today began to take shape in the 17th and 18th centuries.

One of the pioneers in this field was John Graunt, whose work "Natural and Political Observations Made upon the Bills of Mortality" (1662) is often considered the foundation of demography and vital statistics. Graunt's analysis of London's mortality records demonstrated the power of statistical analysis in understanding population dynamics and public health issues. His work inspired others, such as William Petty, who coined the term "political arithmetic" to describe the use of quantitative methods in studying social phenomena.

The 19th century saw significant advancements in statistical theory and practice. The Belgian astronomer and statistician Adolphe Quetelet made substantial contributions to the field, applying statistical methods to social sciences and developing the concept of the "average man." Quetelet's work laid the groundwork for modern social statistics and influenced the development of statistical offices across Europe.

In the United States, the decennial census mandated by the Constitution in 1787 marked the beginning of systematic national data collection. The establishment of the Bureau of the Census in 1902 further institutionalized the practice of official statistics in the country. Similarly, in the United Kingdom, the General Register Office, established in 1837, began collecting vital statistics, while the creation of the Central Statistical Office in 1941 centralized the production of official economic statistics.

The 20th century witnessed a rapid expansion and sophistication of statistical systems worldwide. The founding of the United Nations Statistical Commission in 1947 marked a significant milestone in the internationalization of official statistics. This body has since played a crucial role in developing global statistical standards and promoting the use of official statistics for sustainable development.

Technological advancements have revolutionized the field of official statistics. The advent of computers in the mid-20th century dramatically enhanced the capacity to process and analyze large volumes of data. More recently, the digital revolution and the emergence of big data have opened up new possibilities for data collection and analysis, challenging traditional statistical methods and offering opportunities for more timely and granular insights.

However, with these advancements come new challenges. The proliferation of data sources raises questions about data quality, privacy, and the role of official statistics in an era of information abundance. Statistical offices around the world are grappling with these issues, striving to maintain the relevance and reliability of official statistics while adapting to the changing data landscape.

As we move further into the 21st century, the importance of official statistics continues to grow. The adoption of the Sustainable Development Goals (SDGs) by the United Nations in 2015 has underscored the critical role of high-quality, timely, and reliable data in measuring progress towards global development objectives. This has led to increased efforts to strengthen statistical capacities, particularly in developing countries, and to explore innovative data sources and methodologies.

The COVID-19 pandemic has further highlighted the indispensable nature of official statistics. In times of crisis, reliable data becomes even more crucial for informed decision-making. Statistical offices worldwide have had to adapt quickly to provide timely and relevant data to support pandemic response efforts, demonstrating the flexibility and resilience of modern statistical systems.

Looking ahead, official statistics will continue to evolve, driven by technological innovations, changing societal needs, and global challenges. The integration of new data sources, the development of real-time statistics, and the use of artificial intelligence and machine learning in data processing are likely to shape the future of official statistics. However, the fundamental principles of reliability, objectivity, and relevance will remain at the core of official statistics, ensuring their continued importance in shaping our understanding of the world and informing the decisions that affect our collective future.

As we delve deeper into the world of official statistics in the subsequent chapters, we will explore the intricate workings of national and international statistical systems, the various methods of data collection and dissemination, and the wide-ranging applications of official statistics across different sectors. This journey will provide a comprehensive understanding of how official statistics are produced, used, and continually improved to meet the evolving needs of our complex, data-driven world.

Chapter 2: National Statistical Systems

As we delve deeper into the world of official statistics, it becomes crucial to understand the intricate workings of national statistical systems. These systems form the backbone of data collection, analysis, and dissemination within a country, providing policymakers, researchers, and citizens with valuable insights into various aspects of society and the economy. Building upon the foundations laid in the previous chapter, we will now explore the structure, organization, key institutions, and legal frameworks that govern these systems.

The structure and organization of national statistical systems vary from country to country, reflecting their unique historical, political, and administrative contexts. However, certain common elements can be identified across most nations. At the heart of these systems lies a central statistical office, often referred to as the National Statistical Office (NSO) or Bureau of Statistics. This institution serves as the primary agency responsible for coordinating statistical activities, setting standards, and producing official statistics at the national level.

In many countries, the NSO operates under the direct supervision of a government ministry, typically the Ministry of Finance or Planning. This arrangement ensures that the statistical office has access to necessary resources and can align its activities with national priorities. However, it also raises questions about the independence and objectivity of official statistics, a concern that has led some nations to establish their statistical offices as autonomous or semi-autonomous entities.

The centralized model, where a single agency is responsible for most official statistics, is common in smaller countries and those with a history of centralized governance. In contrast, larger nations and federal systems often adopt a decentralized or federated approach, where multiple agencies share statistical responsibilities. The United States, for instance, has a decentralized system with over 100 federal agencies involved in producing official statistics, coordinated by the Office of Management and Budget.

Regardless of the model adopted, effective coordination among various statistical producers is crucial for maintaining consistency and avoiding duplication of efforts. Many countries have established inter-agency committees or councils to facilitate this coordination. These bodies bring together representatives from different ministries and agencies involved in statistical activities to harmonize methodologies, share best practices, and address common challenges.

Beyond the central statistical office and other government agencies, national statistical systems often include a network of regional and local statistical offices. These sub-national entities play a vital role in collecting data at the grassroots level and implementing national statistical programs. They also produce statistics specific to their regions, which are essential for local planning and development initiatives.

The academic community and research institutions form another important component of national statistical systems. Universities and think tanks contribute to the development of statistical methodologies, conduct independent analyses of official data, and often collaborate with statistical agencies on specialized surveys or studies. This partnership between official statisticians and academic researchers helps to enhance the quality and relevance of official statistics while fostering innovation in statistical techniques.

In recent years, many countries have recognized the need to engage the private sector and civil society organizations in their statistical systems. Private companies, particularly those in the technology and data analytics sectors, can provide valuable expertise in data collection and processing techniques. Civil society organizations, on the other hand, can help ensure that official statistics address the needs of diverse population groups and contribute to evidence-based advocacy.

The effective functioning of national statistical systems relies heavily on a robust legal framework. Statistical legislation serves multiple purposes: it defines the mandate and responsibilities of the national statistical office, establishes principles for statistical activities, and provides safeguards for data confidentiality and respondent privacy. A well-crafted statistical law also ensures the professional independence of official statisticians, protecting them from political interference and maintaining public trust in official statistics.

Many countries have updated their statistical legislation in recent decades to address new challenges and opportunities in the data landscape. These revisions often focus on expanding access to administrative data for statistical purposes, regulating the use of new data sources such as big data, and strengthening data protection measures. The legal framework may also define the relationship between the national statistical office and other data producers, establishing mechanisms for coordination and quality control.

International organizations have played a significant role in promoting the development of comprehensive statistical legislation. The United Nations Fundamental Principles of Official Statistics, adopted by the UN General Assembly in 2014, provide a set of core values and best practices for national statistical systems. These principles emphasize the importance of professional independence, impartiality, scientific methods, and transparency in the production and dissemination of official statistics.

The implementation of statistical legislation often involves the establishment of oversight bodies to monitor compliance and advise on statistical matters. In some countries, this role is fulfilled by a National

Statistical Commission or Council, composed of experts from various fields. These bodies serve as a bridge between the statistical system and its users, ensuring that official statistics remain relevant, reliable, and responsive to evolving societal needs.

Funding is a critical aspect of national statistical systems that is often addressed in legal frameworks. Adequate and stable funding is essential for maintaining the quality and continuity of official statistics. Many countries allocate a specific budget for statistical activities through their national budgeting process, while others have established special funds or allow statistical agencies to generate revenue through the sale of publications or services.

As we transition to the next chapter on international statistical systems, it's important to recognize that national statistical systems do not operate in isolation. They are increasingly interconnected, sharing data, methodologies, and best practices across borders. The globalization of economic activities and the rise of transnational challenges such as climate change have underscored the need for comparable and harmonized statistics at the international level. National statistical systems must therefore balance their domestic responsibilities with the demands of international statistical cooperation, a topic we will explore in depth in the following chapter.

Chapter 3: International Statistical Systems

The world of official statistics extends far beyond national borders, with international organizations playing a crucial role in harmonizing statistical practices, setting global standards, and facilitating cross-country comparisons. As we transition from our exploration of national statistical systems, we now turn our attention to the international arena, where collaboration and coordination are paramount in producing reliable and comparable global statistics.

The United Nations Statistical Commission stands at the forefront of international statistical efforts, serving as the highest decision-making body for international statistical activities. Established in 1947, the Commission has been instrumental in shaping the global statistical landscape. It brings together chief statisticians from member states and international organizations to set statistical standards, develop concepts and methods, and promote their implementation at the national and international levels.

The Commission's work is far-reaching and impacts virtually every aspect of official statistics. It oversees the development of the System of National Accounts (SNA), which provides a comprehensive framework for measuring economic activity. The SNA serves as the foundation for calculating Gross Domestic Product (GDP) and other key economic indicators, ensuring that these vital measures are comparable across countries. The Commission also plays a pivotal role in coordinating global statistical initiatives, such as the development and monitoring of indicators for the Sustainable Development Goals (SDGs).

One of the Commission's most significant achievements has been the adoption of the Fundamental Principles of Official Statistics in 1994, which were later endorsed by the United Nations General Assembly in 2014. These principles serve as a universal framework for national and international statistical activities, emphasizing the importance of independence, impartiality, and professional standards in the production of official statistics. As Paul Cheung, former Director of the United Nations Statistics Division, once remarked, "The Fundamental Principles of Official Statistics are to statisticians what the Hippocratic Oath is to medical doctors. They guide our professional conduct and ensure that the statistics we produce are trustworthy and serve the public good."

The World Bank and the International Monetary Fund (IMF) are two other key players in the international statistical system, each bringing unique contributions to the global statistical community. The World Bank, through its Development Data Group, collects and disseminates a vast array of development indicators, covering topics from poverty and inequality to education and health. These indicators are crucial for policymakers, researchers, and development practitioners worldwide, providing a comprehensive picture of global development trends.

The World Bank's statistical initiatives go beyond mere data collection. They actively work to strengthen statistical capacity in developing countries through technical assistance and training programs. The Bank's Statistical Capacity Building program, for instance, helps countries improve their ability to produce, analyze, and use high-quality statistics for evidence-based decision-making. This support is critical in ensuring that all countries, regardless of their level of development, can participate fully in the global statistical system.

The IMF, on the other hand, focuses primarily on economic and financial statistics. Its Statistics Department works closely with member countries to improve the quality and consistency of macroeconomic statistics. The IMF's Data Standards Initiatives, which include the Special Data Dissemination Standard (SDDS) and the General Data Dissemination System (GDDS), have been instrumental in promoting transparency and encouraging countries to publish timely and comprehensive economic and financial data.

The IMF also plays a crucial role in developing and promoting international statistical standards. For example, the Balance of Payments and International Investment Position Manual, now in its sixth edition, provides a comprehensive conceptual framework for statistics on the transactions and positions between an economy and the rest of the world. As former IMF Managing Director Christine Lagarde once stated, "Good data and good analysis are the lifeblood of good policy. Without them, we are flying blind."

While the United Nations, World Bank, and IMF are perhaps the most visible actors in the international statistical system, numerous other organizations contribute significantly to this global effort. Regional bodies such as Eurostat (the statistical office of the European Union), the Economic Commission for Latin America and the Caribbean (ECLAC), and the African Development Bank play crucial roles in coordinating statistical activities within their respective regions.

The Organization for Economic Cooperation and Development (OECD) is another key player, particularly in the realm of economic statistics. The OECD's statistics cover a wide range of topics, from national accounts and short-term economic indicators to structural business statistics and productivity measures. The organization is also at the forefront of efforts to measure well-being and progress beyond GDP, through initiatives like the Better Life Index.

Amidst this complex network of international statistical organizations, the International Statistical Institute (ISI) holds a unique position. Founded in 1885, the ISI is one of the oldest scientific associations operating in the modern world. Unlike the other organizations mentioned, which are primarily intergovernmental bodies, the ISI is a professional association of statisticians from academia, official statistics, and the private sector.

The ISI plays a crucial role in advancing statistical science and its application through various activities. It organizes the biennial World Statistics Congress, which serves as a global forum for statisticians to exchange ideas and discuss the latest developments in statistical theory and practice. The Institute also publishes several respected journals, including the International Statistical Review and Stat, which contribute to the dissemination of statistical knowledge and research.

One of the ISI's most important contributions to the international statistical system is its work in statistical capacity building, particularly in developing countries. Through its Statistical Capacity Building Committee, the ISI organizes workshops, webinars, and other training activities to help statisticians in these countries enhance their skills and keep up with the latest methodological developments. As former ISI President Pedro Silva once noted, "Building statistical capacity is not just about transferring technical skills. It's about empowering countries to produce and use statistics effectively for their own development."

The ISI also plays an advocacy role for the statistical profession, promoting the importance of statistics in society and working to enhance public understanding of statistics. Its Declaration on Professional Ethics, first adopted in 1985 and regularly updated since then, provides ethical guidelines for statisticians worldwide, complementing the UN Fundamental Principles of Official Statistics.

The interplay between these various international statistical organizations creates a rich ecosystem that supports the production and dissemination of high-quality, comparable statistics at the global level. However, this system is not without its challenges. One of the most pressing issues is the need to harmonize statistical concepts and methods across countries with vastly different economic structures, cultural contexts, and statistical capacities.

Take, for example, the challenge of measuring the informal economy. In many developing countries, a significant portion of economic activity occurs in the informal sector, which is often not fully captured by traditional statistical methods. The international statistical community has had to grapple with how to measure and account for this activity in a way that allows for meaningful cross-country comparisons while still reflecting the realities of individual economies.

Another significant challenge is keeping pace with rapid technological and social changes. The rise of the digital economy, for instance, has posed new questions about how to measure economic activity in an increasingly intangible world. Similarly, the growing importance of issues like climate change and sustainability has led to calls for new types of statistics that can better capture environmental and social progress.

Data privacy and security represent yet another crucial concern in the international statistical system. As data collection and sharing become increasingly global, ensuring the confidentiality of individual and business information while still allowing for the production of detailed statistics has become a complex balancing act. International organizations play a key role in developing guidelines and best practices to address these challenges.

Despite these challenges, the international statistical system continues to evolve and adapt. Recent years have seen a growing emphasis on the use of new data sources, including big data and administrative data, to complement traditional statistical methods. There's also an increasing focus on data interoperability and the development of integrated statistical systems that can provide a more holistic view of social, economic, and environmental issues.

As we look to the future, the importance of international statistical systems is only likely to grow. In an increasingly interconnected world, the need for reliable, comparable global statistics has never been greater. Whether it's tracking progress towards the Sustainable Development Goals, monitoring global economic trends, or addressing transnational challenges like climate change, international statistical systems will continue to play a vital role in informing policy and decision-making at all levels.

As we conclude our exploration of international statistical systems, we can appreciate the complex web of organizations and initiatives that work together to produce the global statistics we often take for granted. From the high-level coordination provided by the UN Statistical Commission to the technical standards set by specialized agencies and the professional development fostered by organizations like the ISI, each component plays a crucial role in this global statistical ecosystem.

In the next chapter, we will delve into the various uses of official statistics, examining how these carefully collected and compiled data inform decision-making across a wide range of sectors, from economic planning to social policy formulation and business strategy. We'll see how the work of national and international statistical systems translates into practical applications that shape our world in countless ways.

Chapter 4: Uses of Official Statistics

Economic planning and development forms the cornerstone of any nation's growth strategy, and official statistics play a pivotal role in this process. Governments, policymakers, and economists rely heavily on these statistics to make informed decisions that shape the economic landscape of a country. The use of official statistics in economic planning is not a recent phenomenon; it has been a fundamental aspect of governance for centuries. However, the sophistication and breadth of these statistics have evolved significantly over time, providing a more comprehensive and nuanced view of economic realities.

At its core, economic planning involves the allocation of resources to achieve specific growth targets and development goals. Official statistics serve as the empirical foundation upon which these plans are built. They provide a quantitative snapshot of the current economic situation, allowing planners to identify areas of strength and weakness within the economy. For instance, Gross Domestic Product (GDP) figures, which are among the most widely used official statistics, offer a broad measure of a country's economic output. By analyzing GDP trends over time, policymakers can gauge the overall health of the economy and make projections for future growth.

Moreover, official statistics break down economic activity by sectors, enabling a more granular understanding of where growth is occurring or stagnating. This sectoral analysis is crucial for targeted interventions and policy formulation. For example, if official statistics reveal a decline in manufacturing output, the government might implement policies to boost industrial production, such as offering tax incentives or investing in infrastructure that supports manufacturing activities.

The use of official statistics extends beyond simple trend analysis. Economists and planners employ sophisticated modeling techniques that rely on these statistics to simulate the potential impacts of different policy choices. These econometric models can predict how changes in one area of the economy might affect others, allowing for more informed decision-making. As Nobel laureate economist Paul Samuelson once noted, "I don't care who writes a nation's laws, if I can write its economics textbooks." This quote underscores the power of economic analysis, which is fundamentally based on official statistics, in shaping policy and, by extension, the future of nations.

In the realm of development planning, official statistics are equally indispensable. They provide the metrics by which progress towards development goals is measured. International organizations like the United Nations use a wide array of statistics to track global development initiatives such as the Sustainable Development Goals (SDGs). These statistics cover everything from poverty rates and educational attainment to environmental indicators and gender equality measures. By standardizing these metrics across countries, official statistics enable comparative analysis and facilitate the sharing of best practices in development strategies.

The role of official statistics in social policy formulation cannot be overstated. Social policies are designed to address societal issues and improve the overall quality of life for citizens. These policies cover a broad spectrum of areas including healthcare, education, housing, and social welfare. To craft effective social policies, policymakers need a clear understanding of the current social landscape, which is where official statistics come into play.

Demographic statistics, for instance, are fundamental to social policy planning. They provide information on population size, age structure, and distribution, which are crucial for planning everything from school systems to healthcare facilities. Birth rates, mortality rates, and life expectancy figures inform policies related to family planning, public health initiatives, and pension systems. As societies age, particularly in developed countries, these demographic statistics become increasingly important for addressing the challenges associated with an aging population.

Education statistics offer another prime example of how official data inform social policy. Enrollment rates, literacy levels, and educational attainment figures help policymakers identify gaps in the education system and allocate resources accordingly. If statistics show low enrollment rates in certain regions or among specific demographic groups, targeted interventions can be designed to address these disparities. Similarly, employment statistics, including unemployment rates and labor force participation rates, guide the formulation of job creation policies and workforce development programs.

Health statistics are equally crucial in shaping public health policies. Data on disease prevalence, mortality causes, and healthcare access inform decisions about healthcare resource allocation, disease prevention programs, and health insurance policies. During public health crises, such as the recent global pandemic, the importance of timely and accurate health statistics becomes even more apparent. As Dr. Tedros Adhanom Ghebreyesus, Director-General of the World Health Organization, stated, "You can't fight a virus if you don't know where it is. That means robust surveillance to find, isolate, test and treat every case, to break the chains of transmission."

Income and poverty statistics are fundamental to social welfare policies. Measures of income inequality, poverty rates, and social mobility inform policies aimed at reducing economic disparities and providing social safety nets. These statistics help policymakers determine eligibility criteria for various social programs and assess the effectiveness of poverty reduction strategies over time.

The use of official statistics in social policy formulation extends beyond mere problem identification. They also play a crucial role in policy evaluation and refinement. By tracking key social indicators over time, policymakers can assess the impact of implemented policies and make necessary adjustments. This data-driven approach to policymaking allows for more effective and responsive governance.

In the realm of business and market research, official statistics serve as an invaluable resource for companies seeking to understand market dynamics, assess opportunities, and make informed strategic decisions. These statistics provide a macro-level view of economic conditions, consumer behavior, and industry trends that businesses can use to complement their own market research efforts.

One of the primary ways businesses utilize official statistics is in market sizing and potential assessment. Population statistics, combined with income data and consumer expenditure surveys, allow companies to estimate the size of their potential market for various products or services. This information is crucial for businesses considering expansion into new geographic areas or launching new product lines. For instance, a company in the fast-moving consumer goods (FMCG) sector might use official statistics on household consumption patterns to identify promising markets for their products.

Official statistics also play a vital role in demand forecasting. Economic indicators such as GDP growth rates, inflation figures, and employment statistics help businesses predict future demand for their products or services. These macroeconomic indicators provide context for company-specific sales data, allowing for more accurate forecasting. As Peter Drucker, the father of modern management theory, once said, "The best way to predict the future is to create it." While this speaks to the proactive nature of business strategy, it also underscores the importance of having reliable data, including official statistics, to inform that creation process.

Industry-specific statistics are particularly valuable for businesses operating in or considering entering specific sectors. For example, manufacturing companies might closely monitor the Index of Industrial Production to gauge overall sector performance and identify trends. Similarly, businesses in the agricultural sector would find crop production statistics and land use data essential for their planning processes.

In addition to aiding strategic planning, official statistics are crucial for risk assessment and management. Economic indicators help businesses anticipate and prepare for economic downturns or upswings. Labor market statistics inform hiring strategies and wage-setting policies. Price indices assist in pricing decisions and in managing inflationary pressures on costs.

For businesses engaged in international trade, official statistics on trade flows, tariffs, and exchange rates are indispensable. These data help companies identify export opportunities, assess the competitiveness of their products in different markets, and manage currency risks. As globalization continues to connect markets worldwide, the importance of these international economic statistics only grows.

Market researchers also rely heavily on official statistics to provide context and validation for their primary research findings. While companies often conduct their own surveys and data collection efforts, official statistics offer a broader, more representative picture of market conditions. They can be used to benchmark company performance against industry averages or to identify discrepancies that might warrant further investigation.

Moreover, official statistics often form the basis for segmentation strategies in market research. Demographic data, socio-economic classifications, and lifestyle statistics help businesses identify and target specific consumer segments. This targeted approach allows for more efficient marketing strategies and product development efforts.

As we transition to the next chapter, it's important to note that while the uses of official statistics in economic planning, social policy formulation, and business research are vast and varied, the reliability of these statistics is paramount. The effectiveness of any decision-making process based on these statistics hinges on their accuracy and credibility. Therefore, understanding the methods used to ensure the reliability of official statistics is crucial for anyone involved in their interpretation and application. The next chapter will delve into the quality assurance methods, accuracy measures, and approaches to dealing with errors and biases in official statistics, providing a comprehensive view of how statistical agencies work to maintain the integrity of the data upon which so many important decisions are based.

Chapter 5: Reliability of Official Statistics

Quality assurance methods

Official statistics form the backbone of evidence-based decision-making in governments, businesses, and international organizations. However, the effectiveness of these decisions hinges on the reliability of the statistical data. Quality assurance methods play a crucial role in ensuring that official statistics maintain the highest standards of accuracy, consistency, and relevance. These methods encompass a wide range of practices and procedures designed to identify, prevent, and correct errors throughout the statistical production process.

One of the fundamental quality assurance methods employed in official statistics is the implementation of standardized procedures. Statistical agencies develop and adhere to rigorous protocols for data collection, processing, and analysis. These standardized procedures help minimize human error and ensure consistency across different surveys and time periods. For instance, the United States Census Bureau employs a comprehensive quality assurance program that includes detailed manuals, training programs, and supervisory reviews at each stage of the data collection and processing cycle.

Another critical quality assurance method is the use of metadata. Metadata, often described as "data about data," provides essential information about the statistical data, including its source, methodology, definitions, and limitations. By maintaining comprehensive metadata, statistical agencies enable users to assess the quality and suitability of the data for their specific needs. The European Statistical System, for example, has developed a Common Metadata Framework that standardizes metadata across European Union member states, enhancing the comparability and interpretability of official statistics.

Cross-validation is another powerful quality assurance technique widely used in official statistics. This method involves comparing data from different sources or methodologies to identify discrepancies and validate results. For example, population estimates derived from administrative records might be cross-checked against survey data or census results. The United Kingdom's Office for National Statistics regularly conducts cross-validation exercises, comparing its labor market statistics derived from household surveys with those obtained from employer surveys and administrative data.

In recent years, the advent of big data and advanced analytics has introduced new quality assurance methods to official statistics. Machine learning algorithms can be employed to detect anomalies and outliers in large datasets, flagging potential errors for human review. Statistical agencies are also exploring the use of artificial intelligence to automate quality checks and improve the efficiency of data validation processes. The Italian National Institute of Statistics (Istat) has been at the forefront of implementing these innovative approaches, developing AI-powered tools for data editing and imputation.

Peer review and external audits constitute another layer of quality assurance in official statistics. Many national statistical offices subject their methodologies and outputs to scrutiny by independent experts or international organizations. The International Monetary Fund's Data Quality Assessment Framework (DQAF) is a widely recognized tool for assessing the quality of official statistics across countries. Through such external evaluations, statistical agencies can identify areas for improvement and align their practices with international standards.

Accuracy and precision measures

Accuracy and precision are fundamental concepts in assessing the reliability of official statistics. While often used interchangeably in casual conversation, these terms have distinct meanings in the context of statistical quality. Accuracy refers to how close a measured value is to the true value, while precision relates to the consistency or reproducibility of measurements. Both aspects are crucial in ensuring the reliability of official statistics.

Statistical agencies employ various measures to quantify and report on the accuracy of their data. One common approach is the calculation of standard errors, which provide an estimate of the variability in a statistic due to sampling. For instance, when reporting unemployment rates, many statistical offices include the standard error alongside the point estimate. This practice allows users to construct confidence intervals and make informed judgments about the reliability of the reported figures.

The coefficient of variation (CV) is another widely used measure of accuracy in official statistics. The CV expresses the standard error as a percentage of the estimate, providing a standardized measure of relative precision. Statistical agencies often use CV thresholds to determine whether estimates are sufficiently reliable for publication. For example, Statistics Canada uses a tiered system where estimates with a CV of 16.5% or less are considered reliable for general use, while those with higher CVs are flagged with warnings or suppressed entirely.

In addition to these quantitative measures, statistical agencies also employ qualitative assessments of accuracy. These may include expert reviews, comparisons with alternative data sources, or historical trend analyses. The Australian Bureau of Statistics, for instance, publishes quality declarations for its major statistical products, providing users with detailed information on the strengths and limitations of the data, including potential sources of error and bias.

Precision in official statistics is often evaluated through measures of reproducibility and consistency. One approach is the use of split-sample techniques, where a dataset is divided into subsamples, and estimates are calculated independently for each. The degree of agreement between these estimates provides insight into the precision of the measurement process. Longitudinal studies, which track the same individuals or entities over time, offer another means of assessing precision by examining the consistency of responses across survey waves.

The concept of total survey error provides a comprehensive framework for understanding and quantifying both accuracy and precision in official statistics. This approach considers all potential sources of error in the survey process, from sampling and coverage errors to measurement and processing errors. By systematically evaluating each error component, statistical agencies can identify areas for improvement and provide users with a more nuanced understanding of data quality.

It's important to note that the pursuit of extreme accuracy and precision must be balanced against practical considerations such as cost, timeliness, and respondent burden. Statistical agencies often face trade-offs between these factors and must make informed decisions about resource allocation. As former U.S. Census Bureau Director Robert Groves noted, "The goal is not perfect data, but data fit for use."

Dealing with errors and biases

Despite rigorous quality assurance methods and careful measurement, errors and biases are an inevitable part of statistical production. The key to maintaining the reliability of official statistics lies in effectively identifying, quantifying, and mitigating these issues. Statistical agencies employ a range of strategies to deal with errors and biases at various stages of the data lifecycle.

One of the primary sources of error in official statistics is sampling error, which arises when inferences are made about a population based on a sample. While sampling error cannot be eliminated entirely, it can be minimized through careful sample design and quantified through measures such as standard errors and confidence intervals. Statistical agencies often use complex sampling techniques, such as stratified and cluster sampling, to improve the precision of estimates while managing costs.

Non-sampling errors, which include issues such as coverage error, non-response bias, and measurement error, present a more complex challenge. Coverage error occurs when the sampling frame does not accurately represent the target population. To address this, statistical agencies invest considerable resources in maintaining and updating their sampling frames. For instance, the U.S. Census Bureau conducts ongoing research to improve its Master Address File, which serves as the basis for many national surveys.

Non-response bias is another significant concern in official statistics, particularly as survey response rates have declined in many countries. Statistical agencies employ various techniques to mitigate this issue, including weighting adjustments, imputation methods, and the use of administrative data to supplement survey information. The UK Office for National Statistics, for example, has developed sophisticated weighting procedures for its Labour Force Survey to adjust for differential non-response across demographic groups.

Measurement error, which occurs when respondents provide inaccurate or incomplete information, is addressed through careful questionnaire design, interviewer training, and data validation procedures. Cognitive testing of survey instruments helps identify potential sources of confusion or misinterpretation. Additionally, statistical agencies often conduct reinterview studies to assess the reliability of responses and quantify measurement error.

Biases in official statistics can arise from various sources, including questionnaire wording, interviewer effects, and social desirability bias. To combat these issues, statistical agencies employ techniques such as randomized question ordering, computer-assisted interviewing, and the use of administrative data for validation. The European Statistical System has developed guidelines for reducing bias in official statistics, emphasizing the importance of neutrality in data collection and analysis.

In recent years, there has been growing recognition of the potential for algorithmic bias in official statistics, particularly as agencies increasingly incorporate big data and machine learning techniques. To address this, statistical offices are developing ethical guidelines for the use of artificial intelligence and implementing rigorous testing procedures to detect and mitigate algorithmic biases. The United Nations Statistical Commission has established a working group on big data for official statistics, which is developing best practices for ensuring fairness and transparency in the use of advanced analytics.

The treatment of outliers presents another challenge in maintaining the reliability of official statistics. While extreme values can significantly impact aggregate measures, they may also represent genuine phenomena of interest. Statistical agencies must strike a balance between mitigating the influence of potential errors and preserving important information. Many offices employ robust statistical techniques, such as winsorization or trimming, to handle outliers while documenting their approach to ensure transparency.

Transparency in error reporting is crucial for maintaining public trust in official statistics. Many statistical agencies publish quality reports alongside their data releases, detailing known limitations, potential sources of error, and measures of uncertainty. The Italian National Institute of Statistics (Istat) has implemented a comprehensive quality reporting system that provides users with detailed information on the accuracy, coherence, and comparability of its statistical products.

Continuous improvement in error mitigation strategies is essential as the landscape of official statistics evolves. The increasing availability of alternative data sources, such as administrative records and big data, offers new opportunities for error reduction but also introduces new challenges. Statistical agencies are investing in research and development to adapt their error mitigation strategies to these changing circumstances.

As we transition to the next chapter on data collection methods, it's important to recognize that the reliability of official statistics is intimately connected to the quality of the underlying data collection processes. The strategies for dealing with errors and biases must be integrated into every stage of statistical production, from survey design to data dissemination. By maintaining a commitment to transparency, continuous improvement, and methodological rigor, statistical agencies can ensure that official statistics remain a trustworthy foundation for decision-making in an increasingly data-driven world.

Chapter 6: Data Collection Methods

The foundation of any robust statistical system lies in its ability to gather accurate and comprehensive data. As we transition from the previous chapter's discussion on the reliability of official statistics, we now delve into the various methods employed to collect this crucial information. Data collection is a complex and multifaceted process that has evolved significantly over time, adapting to technological advancements and changing societal structures. In this chapter, we will explore three primary methods of data collection: surveys and censuses, administrative data sources, and the emerging field of big data and new data sources.

Surveys and Censuses

Surveys and censuses have long been the backbone of official statistics, providing a structured and systematic approach to gathering information about populations, economies, and societies. These methods, while distinct in their scope and frequency, share the common goal of collecting comprehensive data to inform policy decisions and track societal trends.

Censuses are typically large-scale operations that aim to count and gather information about every member of a defined population. The most well-known example is the population census, which is conducted in most countries every five or ten years. The United Nations defines a population census as "the total process of collecting, compiling, evaluating, analysing and publishing or otherwise disseminating demographic, economic and social data pertaining, at a specified time, to all persons in a country or in a well-delimited part of a country."

The comprehensive nature of censuses makes them invaluable sources of baseline data. They provide a complete snapshot of a population at a given point in time, offering insights into demographic characteristics, housing conditions, education levels, and employment status, among other variables. This information is crucial for government planning, resource allocation, and the formulation of targeted policies.

However, the scale and complexity of censuses present significant challenges. They are resource-intensive endeavors, requiring substantial financial investment, extensive human resources, and meticulous planning. The logistics of reaching every household in a country, especially in remote or difficult-to-access areas, can be daunting. Moreover, the time required to process and analyze the vast amount of data collected means that census results may not be available for several years after the data collection phase.

Surveys, on the other hand, offer a more flexible and frequent approach to data collection. Unlike censuses, surveys typically focus on a representative sample of the population rather than attempting to cover everyone. This approach allows for more frequent data collection and the ability to explore specific topics in greater depth.

There are various types of surveys employed in official statistics. Cross-sectional surveys provide a snapshot of a population at a single point in time, while longitudinal surveys follow the same group of respondents over an extended period, allowing for the analysis of changes and trends. Panel surveys, a specific type of longitudinal survey, involve repeated observations of the same variables over time, providing insights into dynamic processes and causal relationships.

The design of surveys requires careful consideration of sampling methodologies to ensure that the selected sample accurately represents the broader population. Probability sampling techniques, such as simple random sampling, stratified sampling, and cluster sampling, are commonly used to minimize bias and maximize the generalizability of results.

The mode of data collection in surveys has evolved significantly with technological advancements. Traditional face-to-face interviews and paper questionnaires have been increasingly supplemented or replaced by telephone interviews, online surveys, and computer-assisted personal interviewing (CAPI) systems. Each mode has its advantages and challenges, and the choice often depends on factors such as the target population, the nature of the information sought, and available resources.

One of the key strengths of surveys is their ability to gather information on subjective experiences, attitudes, and behaviors that may not be captured through other data collection methods. For instance, surveys on consumer confidence, political opinions, or quality of life provide valuable insights that complement more objective economic and social indicators.

However, surveys are not without their limitations. Response rates have been declining in many countries, potentially introducing bias if non-respondents differ systematically from respondents. Additionally, the accuracy of survey data can be affected by factors such as recall bias, social desirability bias, and question wording effects.

Despite these challenges, surveys and censuses remain indispensable tools in the arsenal of official statisticians. Their ability to provide structured, representative data on a wide range of topics makes them essential for evidence-based policymaking and social research. As noted by Sir John Cleland, a renowned demographer, "Surveys are our eyes and ears. They allow us to see and hear what is happening in society, to measure change, and to understand the complex interplay of social, economic, and demographic factors."

Administrative Data Sources

While surveys and censuses are designed specifically for statistical purposes, administrative data sources offer a wealth of information collected as a byproduct of various administrative processes. These sources have gained increasing prominence in official statistics due to their potential to provide timely, cost-effective, and comprehensive data.

Administrative data refers to information collected by government departments and other organizations for the purpose of registration, transaction, or record-keeping, usually during the delivery of a service. Examples include tax records, social security data, health records, educational data, and business registrations. The use of administrative data for statistical purposes represents a shift from primary data collection to the repurposing of existing data.

One of the primary advantages of administrative data is its potential for complete coverage of the relevant population. For instance, tax records typically cover all individuals and businesses required to pay taxes, providing a comprehensive picture of income distribution and economic activity. This level of coverage can be particularly valuable for studying small subgroups or geographic areas that might be underrepresented in sample surveys.

Administrative data also offers the advantage of timeliness. Since the data is collected continuously as part of ongoing administrative processes, it can provide more up-to-date information than periodic surveys or censuses. This timeliness is particularly valuable for monitoring rapidly changing economic conditions or tracking the immediate impact of policy changes.

Furthermore, the use of administrative data can significantly reduce the cost and respondent burden associated with data collection. By leveraging existing data sources, statistical agencies can minimize the need for separate data collection efforts, thereby reducing costs and the burden on individuals and businesses to respond to multiple surveys.

However, the use of administrative data for statistical purposes is not without challenges. One of the primary concerns is data quality. Administrative data is collected for operational rather than statistical purposes, which means that the definitions, classifications, and quality control procedures may not align perfectly with statistical requirements. Variables of interest to statisticians may be missing or recorded inconsistently across different administrative systems.

Privacy and data protection concerns also present significant challenges in the use of administrative data. The linkage of different administrative datasets or the combination of administrative and survey data raises important ethical and legal questions about data confidentiality and individual privacy rights. Strict protocols and legal frameworks are necessary to ensure that the use of administrative data for statistical purposes does not compromise individual privacy or violate data protection regulations.

Another challenge lies in the potential for changes in administrative procedures or policies to affect the consistency and comparability of data over time. For example, changes in tax regulations might alter the way income is reported, making it difficult to construct consistent time series of income statistics.

Despite these challenges, many national statistical offices are increasingly incorporating administrative data into their statistical production processes. The United Kingdom's Office for National Statistics, for instance, has been at the forefront of this trend, developing methods to integrate administrative data into population estimates and other key statistics.

The effective use of administrative data often requires close collaboration between statistical agencies and the administrative bodies that collect the data. This collaboration can lead to improvements in data quality and consistency across government departments. As noted by Katherine Wallman, former Chief Statistician of the United States, "The integration of administrative data into official statistics represents not just a technical challenge, but a cultural shift in how we think about data collection and use across government."

Big Data and New Data Sources

The digital revolution has ushered in an era of unprecedented data generation, leading to the emergence of big data as a potential source for official statistics. Big data refers to extremely large datasets that may be analyzed computationally to reveal patterns, trends, and associations. These datasets are characterized by their volume, velocity (the speed at which new data is generated), and variety (the range of data types and sources).

The potential of big data for official statistics lies in its ability to provide granular, real-time information on a wide range of phenomena. Sources of big data relevant to official statistics include social media data, mobile phone data, satellite imagery, sensor data, and transactional data from e-commerce and financial systems.

One of the most promising applications of big data in official statistics is in the area of economic indicators. For example, some statistical offices are exploring the use of scanner data from retail outlets to complement or even replace traditional price collection methods for consumer price indices. This approach can provide more comprehensive and timely price information, capturing a wider range of products and real-time price changes.

Mobile phone data has shown potential for estimating population movements and distributions, which can be particularly valuable in countries where traditional census-taking is challenging due to resource constraints or political instability. A study conducted by the United Nations Global Pulse initiative demonstrated how mobile phone data could be used to estimate population displacement following a natural disaster, providing crucial information for humanitarian response efforts.

Satellite imagery and remote sensing data offer new possibilities for environmental and agricultural statistics. These data sources can provide information on land use, crop yields, and environmental changes at a level of detail and frequency that would be impractical to achieve through traditional survey methods.

Social media data, while often noisy and biased, can provide insights into public sentiment, consumer behavior, and social trends. Some statistical offices are exploring the use of social media data as a complement to traditional measures of well-being and social indicators.

However, the integration of big data into official statistics presents significant challenges. Data quality is a primary concern, as big data sources often lack the structured, controlled nature of traditional statistical data collection. Issues of representativeness and bias are particularly acute, as big data often reflects the activities of specific subpopulations (e.g., social media users) rather than the entire population of interest.

The sheer volume and velocity of big data also present technical challenges in terms of data storage, processing, and analysis. Statistical offices need to develop new capabilities in data science and machine learning to effectively harness these data sources.

Privacy and ethical considerations are paramount when dealing with big data, particularly when it involves personal information or data collected without explicit consent for statistical purposes. Ensuring public trust in the use of these new data sources is crucial for their acceptance as components of official statistics.

Despite these challenges, many statistical offices and international organizations are actively exploring the potential of big data. The United Nations Statistical Commission has established a Global Working Group on Big Data for Official Statistics to promote the use of big data sources and develop guidelines for their integration into statistical systems.

As Enrico Giovannini, former Chief Statistician of the OECD, noted, "Big data represents both an opportunity and a challenge for official statistics. It offers the potential to provide more timely and granular information, but also requires us to rethink our methods, our skills, and our relationship with data providers and users."

The landscape of data collection for official statistics is evolving rapidly, with traditional methods being complemented and sometimes challenged by new approaches and data sources. As we look to the future, the key challenge for official statisticians will be to harness the potential of these new data sources while maintaining the core principles of statistical quality, relevance, and public trust.

The integration of surveys and censuses, administrative data, and big data sources offers the potential for a more comprehensive and timely statistical system. However, this integration also requires careful consideration of methodological, technical, and ethical issues. As we move forward, the field of official statistics must continue to evolve, embracing new technologies and data sources while upholding the fundamental principles of statistical integrity and public service.

In the next chapter, we will explore how the data collected through these various methods is disseminated to users, examining the strategies employed by statistical offices to make their data accessible, understandable, and actionable for a wide range of stakeholders.

Chapter 7: Data Dissemination Strategies

In the previous chapter, we explored the various methods of data collection employed in official statistics. Now, we turn our attention to an equally crucial aspect of the statistical process: the dissemination of collected data. The effective distribution of statistical information is paramount in ensuring that the hard work of data collection and analysis translates into meaningful insights for policymakers, researchers, and the general public.

Publication formats and channels

The landscape of data dissemination has undergone a significant transformation in recent years, driven by technological advancements and changing user expectations. Gone are the days when bulky statistical yearbooks were the primary means of distributing official statistics. Today, national statistical offices (NSOs) employ a diverse array of publication formats and channels to reach their target audiences.

One of the most traditional yet enduring formats is the printed report. Despite the digital revolution, many users still prefer the tangibility and permanence of physical publications. These reports often serve as comprehensive references, presenting in-depth analyses and interpretations of statistical data. They are particularly valuable for libraries, academic institutions, and government agencies that require authoritative sources for long-term reference.

However, the digital realm has opened up new avenues for data dissemination that offer unprecedented accessibility and interactivity. Web-based platforms have become the cornerstone of modern statistical dissemination strategies. NSOs now maintain robust websites that serve as central hubs for accessing a wide range of statistical products. These websites typically feature downloadable reports in PDF format, allowing users to access information offline while retaining the benefits of digital distribution.

Interactive databases have emerged as a powerful tool for data dissemination. These platforms enable users to query vast datasets, selecting specific variables and time periods of interest. The flexibility of such systems caters to the diverse needs of different user groups, from casual browsers seeking quick facts to researchers conducting in-depth analyses. For instance, the OECD.Stat platform allows users to explore and download data across various domains, from economic indicators to social statistics.

Social media has also become an integral part of data dissemination strategies. Platforms like Twitter, Facebook, and LinkedIn offer NSOs the opportunity to reach wider audiences and engage with users in real-time. These channels are particularly effective for disseminating key statistical findings, infographics, and announcements about new data releases. The UK's Office for National Statistics, for example, maintains an active presence on social media, regularly sharing bite-sized statistical insights that capture public attention and drive traffic to their more comprehensive resources.

Mobile applications represent another frontier in data dissemination. With the increasing prevalence of smartphones, NSOs are developing apps that provide users with easy access to key statistics on the go. These apps often feature interactive visualizations, push notifications for new data releases, and the ability to customize data views according to user preferences. The Australian Bureau of Statistics' "ABS App" exemplifies this approach, offering users quick access to key economic indicators and census data directly on their mobile devices.

Application Programming Interfaces (APIs) have revolutionized the way developers and data scientists interact with official statistics. By providing programmatic access to datasets, APIs enable the creation of custom applications and data-driven services. This not only enhances the utility of official statistics but also fosters innovation in the private sector. The U.S. Census Bureau's extensive API offerings, for instance, have spurred the development of numerous third-party applications that leverage census data for various purposes, from market research to urban planning.

Data visualization techniques

As the volume and complexity of statistical data continue to grow, the importance of effective data visualization has become increasingly apparent. Visual representations of data can convey complex information quickly and intuitively, making statistics more accessible to a broader audience. Consequently, NSOs are investing heavily in developing sophisticated data visualization techniques to enhance the impact and understanding of their statistical outputs.

Interactive charts and graphs have become staples of modern statistical dissemination. These tools allow users to explore data dynamically, adjusting parameters and viewing different aspects of the dataset with ease. For example, line charts can illustrate trends over time, while bar charts effectively compare values across categories. The ability to hover over data points for detailed information or click to drill down into specific subsets of data adds layers of interactivity that enhance user engagement and understanding.

Geospatial visualization techniques have gained prominence, particularly for statistics with a geographical component. Interactive maps enable users to explore data at various levels of granularity, from national overviews to detailed local statistics. Choropleth maps, where areas are shaded or patterned in proportion to a statistical variable, are particularly effective for displaying regional variations. The Eurostat Statistical Atlas, for instance, offers a rich set of interactive maps that allow users to visualize various socio-economic indicators across European regions.

Infographics have emerged as a powerful tool for communicating statistical information to a general audience. By combining data visualizations with concise text and engaging design elements, infographics can tell compelling stories based on statistical findings. They are particularly effective on social media platforms, where they can quickly convey key messages and encourage sharing. Many NSOs now produce regular infographics to highlight important statistical releases or to explain complex statistical concepts in an accessible manner.

More advanced visualization techniques, such as network diagrams and treemaps, are being employed to represent complex relationships and hierarchical data structures. These visualizations can reveal patterns and insights that might not be immediately apparent in traditional tabular formats. For instance, network diagrams can illustrate trade relationships between countries, while treemaps can effectively display the composition of GDP by sector.

The rise of data journalism has also influenced data visualization practices in official statistics. News organizations increasingly collaborate with NSOs to create interactive data stories that combine statistical insights with journalistic narrative. This approach not only enhances public understanding of statistics but also increases the reach and impact of official data. The BBC's collaboration with the UK's Office for National Statistics on various data-driven stories exemplifies this trend.

Virtual and augmented reality technologies are beginning to make inroads into statistical visualization. While still in their early stages, these technologies offer exciting possibilities for immersive data experiences. Imagine, for instance, walking through a virtual environment where economic indicators are represented as three-dimensional objects, or using augmented reality to overlay local statistics onto real-world locations through a smartphone camera.

Open data initiatives

The open data movement has had a profound impact on the dissemination of official statistics. Open data initiatives aim to make government data freely available to the public, fostering transparency, innovation, and economic growth. For NSOs, embracing open data principles has become a key strategy for maximizing the value and impact of official statistics.

At the heart of open data initiatives is the concept of machine-readability. While PDFs and static web pages have their place, truly open data requires formats that can be easily processed by computers. Common open data formats include CSV (Comma-Separated Values) for tabular data, JSON (JavaScript Object Notation) for structured data, and RDF (Resource Description Framework) for linked data. By providing data in these formats, NSOs enable developers, researchers, and data scientists to easily incorporate official statistics into their analyses and applications.

Open data portals have become central hubs for accessing government data, including official statistics. These platforms typically offer a catalog of available datasets, along with metadata describing the content and structure of each dataset. Advanced search and filtering capabilities help users find relevant data quickly. The European Data Portal, for example, aggregates datasets from across EU member states, providing a single point of access for a vast array of official statistics and other government data.

Licensing is a crucial aspect of open data initiatives. To be truly open, data must be released under terms that permit free use, reuse, and redistribution. Many NSOs have adopted standard open licenses, such as the Creative Commons Attribution License, which allows users to freely use the data while requiring attribution to the original source. Clear and permissive licensing encourages innovation and helps build a vibrant ecosystem around official statistics.

Linked Data principles are being increasingly applied to official statistics as part of open data initiatives. By using standardized identifiers (URIs) and common vocabularies, NSOs can create interconnected webs of statistical data that can be easily navigated and combined with other datasets. This approach enhances the discoverability and interoperability of official statistics, enabling more sophisticated analyses that draw on multiple data sources.

Hackathons and data challenges have become popular ways for NSOs to engage with the developer community and showcase the potential of their open data. These events bring together programmers, designers, and subject matter experts to create innovative applications and visualizations using official statistics. By fostering collaboration and creativity, these initiatives can lead to novel uses of statistical data that might not have been envisioned by the NSOs themselves.

The economic impact of open data initiatives in official statistics is significant. By making high-quality data freely available, NSOs contribute to a data-driven economy where businesses can make more informed decisions, entrepreneurs can develop new products and services, and researchers can conduct more comprehensive analyses. A study by the European Data Portal estimated that the market size of open data in the EU28+ countries could reach €75.7 billion by 2020, with a significant portion of this value derived from official statistics.

However, open data initiatives also present challenges for NSOs. Ensuring data quality, maintaining privacy and confidentiality, and keeping up with evolving technical standards require ongoing investment and expertise. NSOs must also balance the demand for openness with their responsibility to protect sensitive information and maintain public trust.

As we look to the future, the trend towards greater openness and accessibility in official statistics is likely to continue. Emerging technologies such as blockchain may offer new ways to ensure the authenticity and traceability of open statistical data. Meanwhile, the increasing integration of official statistics with other forms of big data will present both opportunities and challenges for open data initiatives.

In conclusion, the dissemination of official statistics has evolved far beyond the simple publication of reports. Today's NSOs employ a diverse array of strategies to ensure that their data reaches and impacts the widest possible audience. From interactive visualizations to open data portals, these approaches are transforming the way society engages with official statistics. As we move into the next chapter, we will explore how these global trends in data dissemination are reflected in the specific context of India's national statistical organization, providing a concrete example of how these strategies are implemented in one of the world's largest and most diverse statistical systems.

Chapter 8: National Statistical Organization of India

As we transition from our exploration of data dissemination strategies, we now turn our attention to a specific national statistical system – that of India. The National Statistical Organization (NSO) of India serves as a prime example of how a large, diverse country organizes its statistical infrastructure to meet the complex needs of policymakers, researchers, and citizens alike.

Structure and functions

The National Statistical Organization of India is the central agency responsible for collecting, analyzing, and disseminating official statistics for the country. It operates under the Ministry of Statistics and Programme Implementation (MoSPI) and is structured to address the multifaceted nature of India's statistical requirements.

At the apex of the NSO is the National Statistical Commission (NSC), which serves as the nodal and empowered body for all core statistical activities in the country. The NSC is supported by various divisions and offices that form the backbone of India's statistical system.

One of the key components of the NSO is the Central Statistics Office (CSO). The CSO is responsible for coordinating statistical activities in the country and for maintaining statistical standards. It plays a crucial role in the compilation of national accounts statistics, conducts economic censuses, and computes important economic indicators such as the Index of Industrial Production and Consumer Price Index.

Another vital arm of the NSO is the National Sample Survey Office (NSSO). The NSSO is renowned for its large-scale sample surveys on various socio-economic subjects. These surveys provide critical data on employment, consumer expenditure, housing conditions, and other aspects of India's social and economic life. The NSSO's work is particularly important in a country where administrative data may be incomplete or unreliable in certain areas.

The Field Operations Division (FOD) of the NSO is responsible for the actual data collection process. With a vast network of field investigators spread across the country, the FOD ensures that surveys are conducted efficiently and data is collected accurately. This division faces unique challenges given India's geographical diversity and the need to reach remote and often inaccessible areas.

In addition to these core divisions, the NSO also includes specialized units such as the Data Processing Division, which handles the enormous task of processing and validating the collected data, and the Survey Design and Research Division, which develops and refines survey methodologies to ensure scientific rigor in data collection.

The structure of the NSO reflects the complex nature of India's federal system. While the central organization provides overall direction and coordination, each state and union territory has its own statistical apparatus. This decentralized approach allows for more targeted data collection and analysis at the sub-national level, while the central NSO ensures consistency and comparability across regions.

Major statistical activities

The NSO undertakes a wide range of statistical activities that form the basis of India's official statistics. These activities are designed to provide a comprehensive picture of the country's socio-economic conditions and to track changes over time.

One of the most significant undertakings of the NSO is the conduct of the Economic Census. This massive exercise, carried out periodically, aims to provide a complete count of all economic establishments in the country. The Economic Census serves as a crucial framework for detailed follow-up surveys and provides valuable insights into the structure of India's economy, particularly the informal sector which is often difficult to capture through other means.

The NSO is also responsible for compiling and publishing the National Accounts Statistics. This complex task involves integrating data from various sources to produce estimates of key economic indicators such as Gross Domestic Product (GDP), National Income, and Savings and Investment rates. The methodology for national accounts compilation in India follows international standards set by the United Nations System of National Accounts, adapted to the specific conditions of the Indian economy.

Another major activity of the NSO is the conduct of the Annual Survey of Industries (ASI). This survey provides detailed information on the organized manufacturing sector, including data on output, employment, capital formation, and productivity. The ASI is a critical source of information for policymakers and researchers studying India's industrial development.

The NSO also plays a crucial role in producing price statistics. It compiles and publishes various price indices, including the Consumer Price Index (CPI) and the Wholesale Price Index (WPI). These indices are essential for measuring inflation, adjusting wages and pensions, and deflating national accounts statistics.

In the realm of social statistics, the NSO conducts large-scale sample surveys on topics such as employment and unemployment, household consumer expenditure, health, education, and housing conditions. These surveys, often conducted as part of the National Sample Survey (NSS), provide invaluable data for social policy formulation and evaluation.

The organization is also responsible for compiling and disseminating environmental statistics, an area of growing importance given increasing concerns about sustainability and climate change. This includes data on natural resources, pollution levels, and environmental degradation.

One of the most ambitious projects undertaken by the NSO in recent years has been the Time Use Survey. This survey aims to measure how individuals allocate their time across various activities, providing insights into unpaid work, leisure patterns, and gender disparities in time use. The results of this survey have significant implications for policies related to work-life balance, gender equality, and social welfare.

Coordination with other government agencies

The effectiveness of the NSO's work depends heavily on its ability to coordinate with other government agencies. This coordination is essential not only for data collection but also for ensuring the relevance and usefulness of the statistics produced.

At the central level, the NSO works closely with various ministries and departments to access administrative data and to understand their statistical needs. For example, collaboration with the Ministry of Finance is crucial for national accounts statistics, while coordination with the Ministry of Labour and Employment is essential for labor force surveys.

The Reserve Bank of India (RBI) is another key partner for the NSO. The RBI provides important financial and monetary statistics, which are integrated with other economic data compiled by the NSO. This collaboration is crucial for producing comprehensive and coherent economic statistics.

At the state level, the NSO coordinates with State Directorates of Economics and Statistics. These state-level bodies play a vital role in collecting data at the grassroots level and in implementing national statistical programs. The NSO provides technical guidance and support to these state organizations to ensure uniformity in statistical standards and methodologies across the country.

The NSO also collaborates with academic institutions and research organizations. These partnerships often involve methodological research, capacity building, and peer review of statistical processes. For instance, the Indian Statistical Institute, a premier institution in the field of statistics, often provides technical expertise to the NSO on complex statistical issues.

International coordination is another important aspect of the NSO's work. The organization represents India in various international statistical forums and contributes to global statistical initiatives. It works closely with international organizations such as the United Nations Statistical Division, the World Bank, and the International Monetary Fund to align India's statistical system with international standards and best practices.

One of the challenges in coordination is ensuring data consistency across different sources. The NSO plays a crucial role in reconciling discrepancies and providing authoritative figures when different agencies produce conflicting statistics. This role is particularly important in a large and complex statistical system like India's, where multiple agencies may be involved in producing statistics on the same subject.

The NSO also faces the challenge of balancing the need for detailed, granular data with the imperative of protecting individual privacy and confidentiality. This requires careful coordination with legal authorities and data protection agencies to ensure that statistical activities comply with privacy laws while still providing useful information for policy-making and research.

In recent years, the NSO has been working towards greater integration of its statistical activities with the broader e-governance initiatives of the Indian government. This involves coordination with agencies responsible for digital infrastructure and data management to leverage new technologies for more efficient data collection and dissemination.

As we conclude our examination of the National Statistical Organization of India, it's clear that this institution plays a pivotal role in the country's development process. By providing reliable and timely statistics, the NSO enables evidence-based policy-making and contributes to informed public discourse on social and economic issues. As we move forward to discuss the National Statistical Commission in the next chapter, we'll see how this oversight body works to further strengthen India's statistical system and ensure its continued relevance and effectiveness in a rapidly changing world.

Chapter 9: National Statistical Commission

The establishment of the National Statistical Commission (NSC) in India marked a significant milestone in the country's efforts to strengthen its statistical system and enhance the quality and credibility of official statistics. As we transition from our discussion of the National Statistical Organization of India, it is crucial to understand the role of the NSC in shaping the landscape of statistical activities in the country.

The genesis of the National Statistical Commission can be traced back to the growing recognition of the need for an independent body to oversee and guide the statistical system in India. In the years leading up to its establishment, there was a growing concern among policymakers, academics, and statisticians about the fragmentation of statistical activities across various government departments and the lack of a coordinated approach to data collection and dissemination. This fragmentation often led to inconsistencies in data, duplication of efforts, and gaps in critical areas of national importance.

The idea of a National Statistical Commission was first proposed in the early 1990s, but it took several years of deliberations and consultations before it finally materialized. The government of India, recognizing the importance of robust statistical systems for evidence-based policymaking, constituted a high-level committee in 2000 under the chairmanship of Dr. C. Rangarajan, a renowned economist and former Governor of the Reserve Bank of India. This committee, known as the National Statistical Commission, was tasked with reviewing the entire statistical system of the country and recommending measures for its improvement.

The Rangarajan Commission, as it came to be known, submitted its report in 2001, which laid the foundation for the establishment of a permanent National Statistical Commission. The report emphasized the need for an apex body to oversee all statistical activities in the country and ensure the integrity and reliability of official statistics. It recommended that the NSC should be established as a statutory body with the necessary authority and independence to fulfill its mandate effectively.

Following the recommendations of the Rangarajan Commission, the government of India established the National Statistical Commission through a resolution on June 1, 2005. The Commission was constituted with a broad mandate to serve as the nodal and empowered body for all core statistical activities in the country. Its establishment was hailed as a landmark decision, reflecting the government's commitment to improving the quality and credibility of official statistics.

The National Statistical Commission was given a wide-ranging mandate that encompassed various aspects of the statistical system. One of its primary responsibilities was to identify the core statistics of national importance and to lay down national policies and priorities relating to the statistical system. This task was crucial in ensuring that the country's statistical activities were aligned with national priorities and development goals.

Another critical function of the NSC was to evolve standard statistical concepts, definitions, classifications, and methodologies in different areas of statistics. This standardization was essential for ensuring consistency and comparability of data across different sectors and over time. By promoting uniform standards, the NSC aimed to enhance the reliability and usefulness of official statistics for policymakers, researchers, and other stakeholders.

The Commission was also entrusted with the task of exercising statistical coordination between ministries, departments, and other agencies of the central government. This coordination was vital in avoiding duplication of efforts and ensuring efficient utilization of resources in statistical activities. By fostering collaboration and synergy among different government agencies, the NSC sought to create a more integrated and coherent statistical system.

One of the most significant aspects of the NSC's mandate was its role in ensuring statistical audit of the data collected by various agencies. This function was crucial in maintaining the quality and integrity of official statistics. The Commission was empowered to conduct periodic reviews of statistical activities and methodologies employed by different agencies and recommend measures for improvement. This statistical audit function served as a critical quality assurance mechanism, enhancing the credibility and reliability of official statistics.

The composition of the National Statistical Commission was designed to ensure a balance of expertise and representation. The Commission consists of a part-time Chairperson, four part-time Members, and an ex-officio Member who is the Chief Statistician of India. The members are chosen from among persons of eminence with wide experience in disciplines such as economics, statistics, planning, social sciences, and data management.

The establishment of the NSC also brought about significant changes in the institutional framework of the statistical system in India. The National Sample Survey Organization (NSSO) and the Central Statistical Organization (CSO), which were previously part of the Ministry of Statistics and Programme Implementation, were placed under the oversight of the NSC. This restructuring was aimed at enhancing the autonomy and professional independence of these key statistical agencies.

Since its inception, the National Statistical Commission has played a crucial role in improving the statistical system of India. It has undertaken several initiatives to enhance the quality and coverage of official statistics, promote the use of modern statistical techniques, and strengthen the statistical capacity of various government agencies. The Commission has also been instrumental in promoting the use of technology in data collection and dissemination, advocating for the adoption of advanced statistical software and data management systems.

One of the significant contributions of the NSC has been its efforts to improve the reliability and timeliness of key economic indicators. The Commission has recommended several measures to enhance the quality of national accounts statistics, price indices, and employment data. For instance, it has advocated for the use of more robust methodologies in calculating the Gross Domestic Product (GDP) and suggested improvements in the collection and compilation of price data for the Consumer Price Index (CPI) and Wholesale Price Index (WPI).

The NSC has also played a pivotal role in promoting transparency and accessibility of official statistics. It has recommended the adoption of open data policies and encouraged government agencies to make statistical data more readily available to the public. This emphasis on data accessibility has not only enhanced the transparency of government operations but has also facilitated research and analysis by academics, think tanks, and other stakeholders.

In recent years, the National Statistical Commission has been at the forefront of addressing emerging challenges in the field of statistics. It has recognized the potential of big data and new data sources in complementing traditional statistical methods. The Commission has been exploring ways to integrate these new data sources into the official statistical system while ensuring data quality and privacy protection.

However, the journey of the National Statistical Commission has not been without challenges. One of the persistent issues has been the need for greater statutory backing to enhance its authority and effectiveness. While the NSC was established through a government resolution, there have been calls to enact legislation to give it statutory status. This would not only strengthen its position but also ensure greater autonomy and independence in its functioning.

Another challenge has been the implementation of the Commission's recommendations. While the NSC has made numerous recommendations for improving the statistical system, the pace of implementation has sometimes been slow due to various administrative and bureaucratic hurdles. This has led to calls for more effective mechanisms to ensure timely implementation of the Commission's recommendations.

Despite these challenges, the National Statistical Commission has undoubtedly made significant contributions to improving the statistical system in India. Its role in promoting professionalism, scientific rigor, and independence in statistical activities has been widely recognized. The Commission has been instrumental in enhancing the credibility and reliability of official statistics, which is crucial for informed decision-making and policy formulation.

As we look towards the future, the role of the National Statistical Commission is likely to become even more critical. In an era of data-driven decision-making, the demand for high-quality, timely, and reliable statistics is only going to increase. The NSC will need to continue evolving and adapting to meet these changing needs and expectations.

The Commission will need to grapple with emerging challenges such as the integration of new data sources, the use of artificial intelligence and machine learning in statistical analysis, and the growing concerns around data privacy and security. It will also need to play a key role in building statistical capacity at all levels of government and promoting statistical literacy among policymakers and the general public.

As we conclude our discussion on the National Statistical Commission, it is clear that its establishment has been a significant step forward in India's journey towards a more robust and reliable statistical system. The Commission's efforts have laid a strong foundation for the future development of official statistics in the country. As we move forward to explore other aspects of India's statistical landscape, including index numbers and their applications, we carry with us the understanding of the crucial role that institutions like the NSC play in shaping the quality and credibility of official statistics.

Chapter 10: Index Numbers: Concepts and Applications

As we delve into the world of index numbers, we transition from the broader organizational aspects of statistical systems to more specific methodologies used in official statistics. Index numbers serve as powerful tools in economic and social analysis, providing a concise way to measure changes in complex sets of data over time. This chapter will explore the various types of index numbers, their construction methods, and their crucial applications in economic analysis.

Types of index numbers

Index numbers are statistical measures designed to show changes in a variable or group of related variables over time. They are essential in quantifying and analyzing trends in various economic and social phenomena. The most common types of index numbers include price indices, quantity indices, and value indices.

Price indices measure the average change in prices over time. The Consumer Price Index (CPI) is perhaps the most well-known example of a price index. It tracks the average price of a basket of goods and services typically consumed by households. The CPI is widely used as a measure of inflation and plays a crucial role in economic policy-making. Another important price index is the Wholesale Price Index (WPI), which measures price changes at the wholesale level before goods reach consumers.

Quantity indices, on the other hand, measure changes in the physical volume of goods or services produced or consumed. The Index of Industrial Production (IIP) is a prime example of a quantity index, tracking changes in the volume of industrial output across various sectors of the economy. Quantity indices are invaluable in assessing economic growth and productivity trends.

Value indices combine both price and quantity changes to measure variations in the total value of goods or services. These indices are particularly useful in international trade statistics, where they can help analyze changes in export or import values over time.

Another important category is the composite index, which combines multiple variables to create a single measure. The Human Development Index (HDI), developed by the United Nations, is a prime example of a composite index. It combines indicators of life expectancy, education, and per capita income to rank countries on their level of human development.

Each type of index number serves specific purposes and provides unique insights into economic and social phenomena. Understanding the distinctions between these types is crucial for their proper interpretation and application in policy-making and research.

Construction methods

The construction of index numbers is a complex process that requires careful consideration of various factors. The choice of construction method can significantly impact the resulting index and its interpretation. There are several methods for constructing index numbers, each with its own strengths and limitations.

The simple aggregate method is the most basic approach to constructing an index number. In this method, the prices or quantities of all items in the index are simply added together for each period and compared to a base period. While straightforward, this method has significant limitations. It does not account for the relative importance of different items and can be distorted by items with large absolute values.

To address these limitations, the weighted aggregate method was developed. This approach assigns weights to different items based on their relative importance. The most common weighting scheme is the Laspeyres index, which uses base period quantities as weights. The Laspeyres index is widely used in official statistics, including in the construction of many countries' Consumer Price Indices.

The Laspeyres index formula is given by:

$$P_L = \frac{\Sigma(p_t \; q_0)}{\Sigma(p_0 \; q_0)} \times 100$$

Where p_t is the price in the current period, p_0 is the price in the base period, and q_0 is the quantity in the base period.

An alternative to the Laspeyres index is the Paasche index, which uses current period quantities as weights. The Paasche index tends to give lower results than the Laspeyres index when prices are rising, as it accounts for substitution effects.

The Paasche index formula is:

$$P_P = \frac{\Sigma(p_t \; q_t)}{\Sigma(p_0 \; q_t)} \times 100$$

Where q_t is the quantity in the current period.

To balance the strengths and weaknesses of the Laspeyres and Paasche indices, the Fisher ideal index was developed. This index is the geometric mean of the Laspeyres and Paasche indices and is considered theoretically superior, although it is more complex to calculate.

The Fisher ideal index formula is:

$$P_F = \sqrt{(P_L \times P_P)}$$

In addition to these traditional methods, more advanced techniques have been developed in recent years. The chain-linked index method, for example, updates weights more frequently to better reflect changing consumption patterns. This method is increasingly used in official statistics, including in the calculation of Gross Domestic Product (GDP) by many countries.

The choice of construction method depends on various factors, including data availability, the purpose of the index, and the nature of the phenomenon being measured. Statistical agencies must carefully consider these factors when designing and implementing index numbers.

Uses in economic analysis

Index numbers play a crucial role in economic analysis, providing valuable insights into various aspects of economic performance and social well-being. Their applications span a wide range of fields and inform decision-making at all levels, from individual households to national governments and international organizations.

One of the primary uses of index numbers is in measuring inflation. The Consumer Price Index (CPI) is the most widely used measure of inflation, tracking changes in the cost of living for households. Central banks and governments rely heavily on CPI data to formulate monetary and fiscal policies. For example, many countries use CPI to adjust social security benefits, pensions, and wages to maintain their purchasing power over time.

As noted by economist Paul A. Samuelson, "The CPI is one of the most important and widely used statistics in economics. It affects the income of millions of Americans through automatic wage adjustments called cost-of-living allowances (COLAs)."

Index numbers are also essential in analyzing economic growth and productivity. The Index of Industrial Production (IIP) provides insights into the performance of different industrial sectors, helping policymakers identify areas of strength and weakness in the economy. Similarly, GDP deflators, which are a type of price index, are used to convert nominal GDP into real GDP, allowing for meaningful comparisons of economic output over time.

In the field of international trade, index numbers help in analyzing trends and competitiveness. Terms of trade indices, which compare export price indices to import price indices, provide valuable information about a country's trading position and the relative value of its exports.

Index numbers also play a crucial role in contract negotiations and financial markets. Many long-term contracts include clauses for price adjustments based on specific indices. In financial markets, stock market indices like the S&P 500 or the Dow Jones Industrial Average serve as important benchmarks for investment performance.

In the realm of social statistics, composite indices like the Human Development Index (HDI) provide a more comprehensive measure of societal progress than single indicators like GDP per capita. These indices help policymakers and researchers assess the overall well-being of populations and compare development levels across countries.

The use of index numbers extends to environmental economics as well. Environmental quality indices, for instance, can track changes in air or water quality over time, informing environmental policies and regulations.

However, it's important to note that while index numbers are powerful tools, they also have limitations. As economist Irving Fisher pointed out, "The index number problem is the problem of how to combine many price relatives into one expression of the change in the general price level." This highlights the challenge of accurately representing complex economic phenomena with a single number.

Users of index numbers must be aware of these limitations and interpret the results carefully. Factors such as changes in quality, the introduction of new products, and shifts in consumption patterns can affect the accuracy and relevance of index numbers over time.

Despite these challenges, index numbers remain indispensable tools in economic analysis. They provide a standardized way to measure and compare economic phenomena across time and space, facilitating evidence-based decision-making and policy formulation.

As we conclude our exploration of index numbers, it's clear that they form a fundamental part of the official statistics toolkit. Their ability to distill complex economic and social trends into easily understandable measures makes them invaluable for policymakers, researchers, and the general public alike. In the next chapter, we will turn our attention to a specific domain of official statistics: agricultural statistics. We will examine how these statistics are collected, compiled, and used to inform agricultural policy and food security strategies.

Chapter 11: Agricultural Statistics

As we transition from our discussion on index numbers and their applications in economic analysis, we now turn our attention to a crucial sector that forms the backbone of many economies worldwide: agriculture. Agricultural statistics play a pivotal role in understanding the dynamics of food production, land utilization, and rural economies. This chapter delves into the intricate world of agricultural statistics, focusing on three key areas: crop estimation surveys, land use statistics, and the agricultural census.

Crop estimation surveys are the cornerstone of agricultural statistics, providing essential data on the production and yield of various crops. These surveys are conducted periodically to assess the health and productivity of agricultural lands, offering invaluable insights into food security, economic planning, and policy formulation. The methodology behind crop estimation surveys has evolved significantly over the years, incorporating advanced technologies and statistical techniques to improve accuracy and reliability.

One of the primary methods used in crop estimation surveys is the crop-cutting experiment. This technique involves selecting random plots within a given area and physically harvesting and weighing the produce to estimate yield. Dr. P.V. Sukhatme, a renowned Indian statistician, played a crucial role in developing and refining this method. He once remarked, "The crop-cutting experiment is not merely a statistical exercise; it is a bridge between the farmer's field and the policymaker's desk." This statement encapsulates the profound impact of these surveys on agricultural policy and planning.

The process of conducting crop estimation surveys is complex and multifaceted. It begins with the stratification of the agricultural area based on factors such as soil type, irrigation facilities, and cropping patterns. This stratification ensures that the sample plots selected are representative of the entire region. Trained enumerators then visit these plots at different stages of crop growth, recording observations on plant health, pest infestations, and expected yield.

In recent years, remote sensing technology has revolutionized crop estimation surveys. Satellite imagery and drone-based surveillance provide a bird's-eye view of vast agricultural landscapes, allowing for rapid assessment of crop conditions and early detection of potential issues. This technological advancement has greatly enhanced the timeliness and accuracy of crop estimates, enabling more responsive agricultural policies and interventions.

However, the integration of traditional field-based methods with modern remote sensing techniques is not without challenges. Issues of data calibration, interpretation of satellite imagery, and the need for ground-truthing continue to occupy researchers and statisticians in the field. As one agricultural economist put it, "The marriage of boots-on-the-ground surveys and eyes-in-the-sky technology is the future of crop estimation, but like any marriage, it requires patience, understanding, and continuous effort to make it work."

Moving beyond crop estimation, land use statistics form another critical component of agricultural statistics. These statistics provide a comprehensive picture of how land resources are allocated across different uses, including cultivation, forestry, pastures, and non-agricultural purposes. The importance of land use statistics cannot be overstated in an era of increasing pressure on land resources due to population growth, urbanization, and climate change.

The collection of land use statistics involves a combination of cadastral surveys, remote sensing, and field verification. Cadastral surveys, which involve the detailed mapping and recording of land parcels, form the foundation of land use statistics in many countries. These surveys provide information on land ownership, boundaries, and primary use. However, the maintenance and updating of cadastral records can be a Herculean task, especially in countries with complex land tenure systems and rapid land use changes.

Remote sensing has emerged as a powerful tool in supplementing and verifying cadastral records. Satellite imagery, when analyzed using geographic information systems (GIS), can provide up-to-date information on land cover and use patterns over large areas. This is particularly valuable in monitoring changes in forest cover, agricultural expansion, and urban sprawl. As one land use expert noted, "Satellite imagery gives us the big picture, but it's the integration with ground-level data that brings that picture into focus."

The classification of land use categories is a critical aspect of land use statistics. International organizations like the Food and Agriculture Organization (FAO) have developed standardized classification systems to ensure comparability of land use data across countries. These classifications typically include categories such as arable land, permanent crops, permanent meadows and pastures, forests, and built-up areas. However, the application of these classifications can be challenging in areas with mixed land uses or traditional agricultural systems that don't neatly fit into predefined categories.

Land use statistics play a crucial role in informing agricultural and environmental policies. They help in identifying trends in land degradation, monitoring the expansion of cultivated areas, and assessing the impact of land use changes on biodiversity and ecosystem services. In the words of a prominent agronomist, "Land use statistics are the silent sentinels of our changing landscapes, alerting us to transformations that might otherwise go unnoticed until it's too late to act."

The third pillar of agricultural statistics discussed in this chapter is the agricultural census. Unlike the more frequent crop estimation surveys, the agricultural census is a comprehensive enumeration of all agricultural holdings in a country, typically conducted every five or ten years. It provides a snapshot of the structure of the agricultural sector, including information on farm size, crop diversification, livestock holdings, and the socio-economic characteristics of farming households.

The history of agricultural censuses dates back to ancient civilizations, where rulers conducted rudimentary counts of livestock and grain stores. In modern times, the FAO has played a leading role in promoting and standardizing agricultural censuses worldwide through its World Programme for the Census of Agriculture. This program provides guidelines and methodologies for conducting agricultural censuses, ensuring a degree of international comparability while allowing for national adaptations.

The scope of an agricultural census is vast, covering a wide range of topics. These typically include the number and size of agricultural holdings, land tenure, land use and crop area, irrigation, livestock numbers, use of agricultural machinery, and demographic characteristics of agricultural holders. In recent years, there has been a growing emphasis on including questions related to environmental practices, such as soil conservation measures and the use of organic farming techniques.

Conducting an agricultural census is a massive undertaking, requiring extensive planning, resources, and coordination. The process typically begins with the development of a census framework, followed by the design of questionnaires, training of enumerators, and the actual field enumeration. In large countries, the enumeration phase alone can take several months to complete.

One of the key challenges in conducting agricultural censuses is ensuring complete coverage, especially in remote and inaccessible areas. innovative approaches have been developed to address this challenge. For instance, some countries have experimented with using satellite imagery to identify agricultural holdings in remote areas, which are then visited by enumerators. Others have explored the use of mobile technology and tablet-based data collection to improve the efficiency and accuracy of the enumeration process.

The data collected through agricultural censuses serve multiple purposes. At the national level, they inform agricultural policy and rural development strategies. As one policymaker put it, "The agricultural census is our compass in navigating the complex terrain of rural development. It tells us where we are and helps us chart a course for where we want to go." At a more localized level, census data are used for planning agricultural extension services, targeting subsidies, and designing interventions to improve agricultural productivity.

Moreover, agricultural census data play a crucial role in the construction of sampling frames for more frequent agricultural surveys. The comprehensive nature of the census provides a reliable basis for designing sample surveys that can provide more timely and specific information on various aspects of agriculture between census years.

In recent years, there has been growing recognition of the potential of agricultural censuses to contribute to broader development goals. For instance, census data can provide valuable insights into issues of food security, rural poverty, and gender dynamics in agriculture. As the FAO's Director of Statistics once remarked, "The agricultural census is not just about counting crops and livestock; it's about understanding the lives and livelihoods of rural populations."

However, the conduct of agricultural censuses is not without its challenges. The high cost and complexity of these operations can be prohibitive for many developing countries. There are also concerns about the timeliness of census data, given the long intervals between censuses and the time required for data processing and dissemination. To address these issues, some countries have adopted a modular approach to agricultural censuses, combining a core census with rotating thematic modules conducted more frequently.

As we conclude our exploration of agricultural statistics, it's clear that crop estimation surveys, land use statistics, and agricultural censuses form a trinity of tools that provide a comprehensive understanding of the agricultural sector. Each of these components offers unique insights, from the granular detail of crop yields to the broad sweeps of land use changes and the structural characteristics of farming systems.

The importance of these statistical tools extends far beyond the realm of agriculture. They inform decisions that affect food security, rural livelihoods, environmental sustainability, and economic development. As one agricultural economist eloquently put it, "Agricultural statistics are the seeds from which informed policies grow, nourishing not just our understanding of farming, but our vision for a sustainable and food-secure future."

As we look to the future, the field of agricultural statistics continues to evolve. The integration of big data, machine learning, and Internet of Things (IoT) technologies promises to revolutionize data collection and analysis in agriculture. Precision agriculture techniques, coupled with advanced statistical methods, offer the potential for near real-time monitoring of crop conditions and yields. These developments, while exciting, also raise new challenges in terms of data management, privacy, and the need for new statistical methodologies.

In the next chapter, we will shift our focus to another crucial sector of the economy: industry. We will explore the various statistical tools and surveys used to measure and analyze industrial production, productivity, and growth. The Annual Survey of Industries, Index of Industrial Production, and statistics on small-scale industries will be our guides as we navigate the complex landscape of industrial statistics.

Chapter 12: Industrial Statistics

As we transition from our exploration of agricultural statistics, we now turn our attention to another crucial sector of the economy: industry. Industrial statistics form the backbone of economic analysis and policy-making in the manufacturing and production sectors. These statistics provide invaluable insights into the structure, performance, and growth of industries, enabling policymakers, economists, and business leaders to make informed decisions.

Annual Survey of Industries

The Annual Survey of Industries (ASI) is the cornerstone of industrial statistics in many countries, including India. This comprehensive survey provides a detailed picture of the organized manufacturing sector, covering factories employing 10 or more workers using power (or 20 or more workers without using power). The ASI collects a wide range of data, including information on capital, employment, wages, input costs, output, and value addition.

The importance of the ASI cannot be overstated. It serves as a primary source of industrial statistics for policy formulation, economic analysis, and academic research. The survey's methodology has evolved over the years to ensure accuracy and relevance. Field investigators visit selected factories, collecting data through a structured questionnaire. The information gathered is then meticulously processed, validated, and aggregated to produce national and regional estimates.

One of the key strengths of the ASI is its ability to provide time-series data, allowing analysts to track trends and patterns in industrial growth over extended periods. This longitudinal perspective is invaluable for understanding structural changes in the economy and evaluating the impact of various policy interventions.

The ASI also plays a crucial role in national accounts compilation. The data collected forms a significant input for estimating the contribution of the manufacturing sector to the Gross Domestic Product (GDP). As noted by renowned economist Dr. C. Rangarajan, "The ASI data is the bedrock on which our understanding of the organized manufacturing sector is built. It provides the granular details needed for evidence-based policymaking in the industrial sector."

However, it's important to acknowledge that the ASI, like any large-scale survey, has its limitations. The survey primarily covers the organized sector, leaving out a significant portion of the unorganized manufacturing activities. This gap has led to ongoing debates about the true representation of the manufacturing sector in official statistics. As a result, many statistical offices are now exploring ways to complement the ASI with other data sources to capture a more comprehensive picture of industrial activity.

Index of Industrial Production

While the ASI provides an annual snapshot of the industrial sector, policymakers and analysts often require more frequent updates on industrial performance. This need is met by the Index of Industrial Production (IIP), a crucial short-term indicator that measures the growth of the industrial sector on a monthly basis.

The IIP is typically constructed as a weighted average of the physical output of a carefully selected basket of industrial products. These products are chosen to represent various segments of the manufacturing, mining, and electricity sectors. The selection of items and their weights is periodically revised to reflect changes in the industrial structure and consumption patterns.

The importance of the IIP lies in its timeliness and frequency. As a monthly indicator, it provides early signals of industrial trends, allowing for quick policy responses to economic fluctuations. Central banks, for instance, closely monitor the IIP when making monetary policy decisions. A sustained decline in the IIP might signal an economic slowdown, potentially warranting monetary easing to stimulate growth.

The construction of the IIP is a complex process that requires meticulous data collection and statistical expertise. Production data is gathered from various sources, including direct returns from factories, administrative records, and industry associations. This data is then aggregated using a weighting scheme that reflects the relative importance of different products and sectors in the overall industrial structure.

One of the challenges in constructing the IIP is ensuring its relevance in a rapidly changing industrial landscape. New products emerge, production technologies evolve, and the relative importance of different industries shifts over time. To address this, statistical offices periodically revise the base year and item basket of the IIP. These revisions aim to capture structural changes in the economy and improve the index's representativeness.

The interpretation of IIP data requires careful consideration of various factors. Seasonal fluctuations, for instance, can significantly impact monthly figures. Many statistical offices publish seasonally adjusted IIP data to facilitate more meaningful month-on-month comparisons. Additionally, one-off events such as strikes, natural disasters, or major policy changes can cause temporary spikes or dips in the index, necessitating a nuanced interpretation of the data.

Despite its limitations, the IIP remains a vital tool for economic analysis and policy-making. As noted by Dr. Pronab Sen, former Chief Statistician of India, "The IIP serves as the economy's pulse, providing crucial real-time information on industrial activity. Its importance in guiding short-term economic management cannot be overstated."

Small-scale Industry Statistics

While the ASI and IIP primarily focus on the organized and larger industrial units, the small-scale industry sector plays a vital role in many economies, particularly in developing countries. This sector often serves as a breeding ground for entrepreneurship, contributes significantly to employment generation, and plays a crucial role in balanced regional development.

Collecting statistics on small-scale industries presents unique challenges. The sheer number of units, their geographical dispersion, and the informal nature of many operations make comprehensive data collection difficult. Despite these challenges, many countries have recognized the importance of small-scale industry statistics and have developed specialized surveys and censuses to capture data from this sector.

In India, for example, the Ministry of Micro, Small and Medium Enterprises conducts periodic censuses of micro, small, and medium enterprises (MSMEs). These censuses aim to provide a comprehensive picture of the MSME sector, covering aspects such as the number of units, employment, output, credit needs, and technological status.

The data collected through these surveys serve multiple purposes. At a policy level, they inform targeted interventions for small-scale industry development. For instance, data on credit accessibility might lead to the formulation of specialized lending programs for small enterprises. Employment data from this sector often reveals important trends in job creation and skill development needs.

One of the key challenges in small-scale industry statistics is the definition and classification of units. The criteria for classifying an enterprise as 'small-scale' often vary across countries and can change over time. In India, for example, the definition of MSMEs has been revised several times, with the most recent change in 2020 introducing turnover-based criteria alongside the traditional investment-based definition.

The informal nature of many small-scale operations poses another challenge for statisticians. A significant portion of these enterprises may operate outside the formal registration and reporting systems, leading to potential underestimation in official statistics. To address this, many countries employ a combination of methods, including area sampling techniques and the use of proxy indicators, to estimate the size and contribution of the informal small-scale sector.

Despite these challenges, the importance of small-scale industry statistics cannot be overstated. As noted by Dr. R. Nagaraj, a prominent Indian economist, "Small-scale industries are the lifeblood of our industrial ecosystem. Accurate statistics on this sector are crucial for understanding employment dynamics, regional disparities, and the overall health of the economy."

The evolution of technology and data collection methods offers new opportunities for improving small-scale industry statistics. Mobile-based surveys, for instance, have shown promise in reaching remote and informal enterprises. Similarly, the integration of administrative data from various government agencies can provide a more comprehensive picture of small-scale industrial activity.

As we look to the future, the importance of industrial statistics is only set to grow. The advent of the Fourth Industrial Revolution, characterized by technologies such as artificial intelligence, the Internet of Things, and advanced robotics, is reshaping the industrial landscape.

This transformation presents new challenges and opportunities for industrial statisticians.

One key area of focus is the measurement of the digital economy. Traditional industrial classification systems and survey methodologies may not adequately capture the nuances of digital products and services. Statistical offices around the world are grappling with questions such as how to measure the output of cloud computing services or how to account for the value created by data in the production process.

Another emerging area is the integration of environmental considerations into industrial statistics. As countries strive to achieve sustainable development goals, there's a growing need for data on industrial energy consumption, emissions, and resource efficiency. Many statistical offices are working on developing 'green' versions of traditional indicators like the IIP to provide a more holistic view of industrial performance.

The COVID-19 pandemic has further underscored the importance of timely and accurate industrial statistics. The disruptions caused by the pandemic highlighted the need for real-time data on industrial activity to inform crisis response and recovery planning. This has accelerated efforts to leverage new data sources, such as satellite imagery and online transactions, to complement traditional survey-based approaches.

As we conclude our exploration of industrial statistics, it's clear that this field is at the intersection of economic analysis, policy-making, and technological innovation. The challenges are significant, but so are the opportunities. As we move forward, the continued evolution of industrial statistics will play a crucial role in our understanding of economic dynamics and our ability to shape a prosperous and sustainable future.

In the next chapter, we will delve into another critical area of official statistics: price statistics. We will explore how indices like the Consumer Price Index and Wholesale Price Index are constructed and used to measure inflation and guide economic policy. This exploration will build on our understanding of industrial statistics, as price movements in industrial goods form a significant component of these broader price indices.

Chapter 13: Price Statistics

As we transition from our discussion on industrial statistics, we now turn our attention to a crucial aspect of economic measurement: price statistics. Price statistics form the backbone of many economic analyses and policy decisions, providing essential insights into inflation, purchasing power, and overall economic health. In this chapter, we will explore three key measures of price statistics: the Consumer Price Index, the Wholesale Price Index, and the GDP deflator.

The Consumer Price Index (CPI) is perhaps the most widely recognized and utilized measure of price changes in an economy. It serves as a barometer for the cost of living, tracking the average change in prices over time that consumers pay for a basket of goods and services. This basket typically includes items such as food, housing, clothing, transportation, and healthcare, among others. The composition of this basket is carefully determined to reflect the spending patterns of the average household in a given country or region.

The calculation of the CPI involves a complex process of data collection and analysis. Statistical agencies regularly survey prices at various retail outlets, gathering information on thousands of items. These prices are then weighted according to their importance in the typical consumer's budget. For instance, housing costs might carry a larger weight than entertainment expenses, reflecting their relative significance in household spending.

One of the primary uses of the CPI is to measure inflation, which is the rate at which the general level of prices for goods and services is rising, consequently eroding purchasing power. Governments and central banks closely monitor the CPI to inform monetary policy decisions. A rising CPI might prompt a central bank to increase interest rates to curb inflationary pressures, while a falling or stagnant CPI could signal the need for economic stimulus measures.

The CPI also plays a crucial role in wage negotiations and social benefit adjustments. Many labor contracts include cost-of-living adjustments (COLAs) tied to changes in the CPI, ensuring that workers' wages keep pace with inflation. Similarly, government programs such as Social Security often use the CPI to adjust benefit payments, protecting recipients from the erosive effects of inflation on their purchasing power.

However, it's important to note that the CPI is not without its limitations and criticisms. One common critique is the potential for substitution bias. As prices of certain goods rise, consumers may switch to lower-priced alternatives, a behavior not immediately captured in the fixed basket of goods used to calculate the CPI. This can lead to an overestimation of inflation. Additionally, the CPI may not adequately reflect quality improvements in products over time, potentially overstating inflation in sectors with rapid technological advancements.

Moving from the consumer perspective to that of producers and wholesalers, we encounter the Wholesale Price Index (WPI). The WPI measures the changes in prices of goods at the wholesale level, before they reach consumers. This index typically includes raw materials, intermediate goods, and finished products sold in bulk quantities.

The WPI serves several important functions in economic analysis. Firstly, it provides an early indicator of inflationary trends in the economy. Since changes in wholesale prices often precede changes in retail prices, the WPI can offer a preview of future consumer price movements. This makes it a valuable tool for policymakers and businesses in anticipating and preparing for economic shifts.

Secondly, the WPI is particularly useful in industries where raw material costs play a significant role. Manufacturing firms, for instance, closely monitor the WPI to gauge changes in their input costs and adjust their pricing strategies accordingly. In some countries, the WPI is used as a deflator for national income accounts, helping to convert nominal values into real terms.

The calculation of the WPI, like the CPI, involves a complex methodology. Prices are collected from various wholesale markets and manufacturers, covering a wide range of commodities. These prices are then weighted based on the relative importance of each commodity in the economy. The weights are typically derived from the value of production or trade volumes of the commodities.

One notable difference between the WPI and CPI is their coverage. While the CPI focuses on final goods and services purchased by consumers, the WPI includes intermediate goods and raw materials. This broader coverage makes the WPI more sensitive to supply-side shocks, such as changes in commodity prices or exchange rates.

However, the WPI also has its limitations. It doesn't capture price changes in the service sector, which forms a significant part of many modern economies. Additionally, the WPI can be more volatile than the CPI due to its sensitivity to commodity price fluctuations, potentially making it a less reliable indicator of long-term inflationary trends.

The third key measure we'll explore in this chapter is the GDP deflator. Unlike the CPI and WPI, which are based on fixed baskets of goods, the GDP deflator is a more comprehensive price index that covers all goods and services produced in an economy. It is derived by dividing the nominal GDP by the real GDP and multiplying by 100.

The GDP deflator is a crucial tool in national income accounting, allowing economists to distinguish between changes in the value of economic output due to price changes and those due to actual increases in production. This distinction is essential for accurately measuring economic growth and productivity.

One of the main advantages of the GDP deflator is its comprehensiveness. It automatically reflects changes in consumption patterns as it's based on the current structure of the economy. This makes it less susceptible to the substitution bias that can affect fixed-basket indices like the CPI.

The GDP deflator also captures price changes in a wider range of goods and services, including those purchased by businesses and the government, not just consumers. This broader coverage makes it a more accurate reflection of overall price changes in the economy.

However, the GDP deflator has its own limitations. It's not as timely as the CPI or WPI, as it's typically calculated quarterly along with GDP figures. Additionally, because it includes prices of exported goods but excludes imported goods, it may not always align closely with the cost of living experienced by domestic consumers.

In practice, economists and policymakers often use a combination of these price indices to get a comprehensive picture of price trends in the economy. Each index offers unique insights and has its own strengths and weaknesses.

For instance, central banks might focus more on the CPI when setting monetary policy, as it directly reflects the inflation experienced by consumers. On the other hand, businesses might pay closer attention to the WPI to anticipate changes in their input costs. Meanwhile, economists analyzing long-term economic trends might rely more heavily on the GDP deflator for its comprehensive coverage.

Understanding these different price statistics is crucial for anyone seeking to comprehend the complexities of modern economies. They provide essential tools for measuring inflation, adjusting for price changes in economic analysis, and informing a wide range of economic decisions.

As we conclude our exploration of price statistics, it's worth noting that the field continues to evolve. Statistical agencies around the world are constantly refining their methodologies to improve the accuracy and relevance of these measures. New data sources, such as online prices and scanner data from retail outlets, are being incorporated to enhance the timeliness and precision of price indices.

In the next chapter, we will delve into the intricate world of national accounts statistics, exploring how countries measure their overall economic performance and structure. We'll examine the System of National Accounts, the calculation of GDP and its components, and the use of input-output tables in economic analysis. This will build upon our understanding of price statistics, showing how these measures feed into the broader picture of national economic accounting.

Chapter 14: National Accounts Statistics

The realm of national accounts statistics stands as a cornerstone in understanding the economic health and performance of a nation. As we delve into this crucial aspect of official statistics, it's important to recognize how it builds upon the concepts of index numbers and various sectoral statistics discussed in previous chapters. National accounts provide a comprehensive framework for analyzing the economic activities within a country, offering invaluable insights for policymakers, economists, and businesses alike.

The System of National Accounts (SNA) serves as the internationally agreed standard for compiling national accounts statistics. Developed collaboratively by the United Nations, the European Commission, the International Monetary Fund, the Organisation for Economic Co-operation and Development, and the World Bank, the SNA provides a set of comprehensive, consistent, and flexible macroeconomic accounts to meet the needs of government and private-sector analysts, policymakers, and decision makers.

The SNA framework is designed to be applicable to all economies, regardless of their level of economic development, institutional arrangements, or complexity. It encompasses a coherent, consistent, and integrated set of macroeconomic accounts, balance sheets, and tables based on internationally agreed concepts, definitions, classifications, and accounting rules. This standardization allows for meaningful comparisons between countries and over time, facilitating a deeper understanding of economic structures and processes.

At its core, the SNA revolves around the concept of economic transactions. These transactions can be broadly categorized into those involving goods and services, distribution transactions, and financial transactions. The system meticulously records these transactions, providing a detailed picture of the flow of economic value within an economy. This comprehensive approach allows for the calculation of key economic indicators, most notably the Gross Domestic Product (GDP).

GDP, often referred to as the "pulse" of an economy, is perhaps the most widely recognized and utilized measure derived from national accounts. It represents the total value of all goods and services produced within a country's borders over a specific period, typically a year or a quarter. The calculation of GDP is a complex process that involves aggregating various components of economic activity.

There are three primary approaches to calculating GDP, each offering a unique perspective on the economy. The production approach, also known as the value-added approach, calculates GDP by summing the value added at each stage of production across all industries in the economy. This method highlights the contribution of different sectors to the overall economic output.

The income approach, on the other hand, measures GDP by adding up all the income earned by factors of production in the economy. This includes wages, profits, rents, and interest payments. The income approach provides insights into how the national income is distributed among different economic agents.

The expenditure approach, perhaps the most commonly used method, calculates GDP by summing all final expenditures in the economy. This includes household consumption, government spending, business investment, and net exports (exports minus imports). The expenditure approach is particularly useful for understanding the drivers of economic growth and the relative importance of different components of aggregate demand.

While GDP is a crucial indicator, it's important to note that national accounts statistics encompass much more than just this single measure. The SNA provides a framework for calculating a wide range of economic indicators, each offering unique insights into different aspects of the economy. For instance, Gross National Income (GNI) adjusts GDP to account for income flows between countries, providing a measure of the total income of a country's residents. Net National Income (NNI) further refines this by accounting for the depreciation of capital assets.

The national accounts also provide detailed breakdowns of economic activity by sector, allowing for in-depth analysis of specific areas of the economy. For example, the accounts might separately report on the output of the manufacturing sector, the services sector, and the agricultural sector. This sectoral analysis is crucial for understanding structural changes in the economy over time and for formulating targeted economic policies.

One of the most powerful tools within the national accounts framework is the Input-Output (I-O) tables. These tables provide a detailed picture of the interdependencies between different sectors of the economy, showing how the output of one industry is used as input in other industries. I-O tables are invaluable for understanding the structure of an economy and for analyzing the potential impacts of economic shocks or policy changes.

The construction of I-O tables is a complex process that requires detailed data on inter-industry transactions. The tables typically show the flows of goods and services between all the individual sectors of an economy over a stated period of time. By providing a comprehensive view of the linkages between different industries, I-O tables allow economists to model how changes in one sector might ripple through the entire economy.

For instance, if there's a significant increase in demand for automobiles, I-O tables can help predict not just the direct effect on the automobile manufacturing industry, but also the indirect effects on industries that supply components to automobile manufacturers, the transportation industry that ships the cars, and even the advertising industry that markets them. This type of analysis is crucial for understanding the full economic impact of various events or policy decisions.

Beyond their use in economic analysis, I-O tables also play a critical role in the compilation of national accounts themselves. They provide a framework for ensuring the consistency and coherence of the accounts, helping to identify and rectify discrepancies in the data. The process of balancing an I-O table – ensuring that the total inputs for each industry match its total outputs – is an important step in validating the overall national accounts.

While national accounts statistics provide an invaluable tool for economic analysis and policy-making, it's important to recognize their limitations. One key challenge is the measurement of the informal economy, which can be significant in many developing countries. Activities in the informal sector, by their nature, are often not captured in official statistics, potentially leading to an underestimation of true economic activity.

Another challenge lies in measuring the quality of goods and services, rather than just their quantity. GDP, for instance, doesn't distinguish between economic activities that enhance well-being and those that might be detrimental. For example, increased spending on pollution cleanup would increase GDP, even though the underlying environmental degradation is not a positive development.

There's also the question of how well GDP and other national accounts measures reflect overall societal well-being. Critics argue that an excessive focus on GDP growth can lead to policies that prioritize short-term economic gains over long-term social and environmental sustainability. This has led to the development of alternative measures, such as the Human Development Index and various measures of "green GDP" that attempt to account for environmental degradation.

Despite these challenges, national accounts statistics remain an essential tool for understanding and managing modern economies. They provide a comprehensive, systematic, and quantitative description of a country's entire economy, its components, and its relations with other economies. As such, they form the backbone of macroeconomic analysis and policy-making.

The future of national accounts statistics is likely to see continued refinement and expansion of the existing framework. There's growing interest in developing more comprehensive measures of economic well-being that go beyond traditional GDP. This includes efforts to better account for non-market activities, such as household production, and to incorporate measures of environmental sustainability and social progress.

Advancements in data collection and processing technologies are also opening up new possibilities for national accounts statistics. Big data and artificial intelligence have the potential to provide more timely and granular economic data, potentially revolutionizing the way national accounts are compiled and analyzed.

As we move forward, the challenge will be to balance the need for continuity and comparability in national accounts statistics with the desire to develop more comprehensive and nuanced measures of economic performance and societal well-being. This evolution of national accounts will be crucial in ensuring that our economic statistics continue to provide relevant and actionable insights in an increasingly complex global economy.

As we conclude our exploration of national accounts statistics, it's worth reflecting on how this field connects to other areas of official statistics. The data and methodologies used in national accounts draw heavily from other statistical domains, including price statistics, labor market statistics, and various sectoral surveys. In turn, the insights provided by national accounts feed into a wide range of other statistical and policy areas. In the next chapter, we'll turn our attention to another fundamental aspect of official statistics: the population census. This crucial statistical undertaking provides the demographic foundation upon which many other statistics, including national accounts, are built.

Chapter 15: Population Census

As we transition from our exploration of national accounts statistics, we now turn our attention to one of the most fundamental and comprehensive data collection efforts undertaken by nations worldwide: the population census. This chapter delves into the intricacies of census methodology, the crucial demographic indicators derived from census data, and the complex socio-economic classification systems that emerge from this monumental statistical endeavor.

The population census stands as a cornerstone of official statistics, providing a snapshot of a nation's demographic landscape at a specific point in time. It serves as the foundation for countless policy decisions, resource allocations, and social research initiatives. The United Nations defines a population census as "the total process of collecting, compiling, evaluating, analyzing and publishing or otherwise disseminating demographic, economic and social data pertaining, at a specified time, to all persons in a country or in a well-delimited part of a country."

Census methodology has evolved significantly since its inception, adapting to technological advancements and changing societal norms. Traditionally, censuses were conducted through door-to-door visits by enumerators who would collect information on standardized forms. This method, while comprehensive, was time-consuming and labor-intensive. In recent decades, many countries have adopted mixed-mode approaches, combining traditional enumeration with postal surveys, online questionnaires, and the use of administrative data.

The planning and execution of a census is a complex undertaking that often spans several years. It begins with the development of questionnaires that must balance the need for comprehensive data collection with the practicalities of field operations and respondent burden. Questions are carefully crafted to ensure clarity and minimize ambiguity, often undergoing extensive testing and piloting before finalization.

One of the most critical aspects of census methodology is achieving complete coverage of the population. This involves meticulous mapping and listing exercises to ensure that every household and individual is accounted for. In many countries, this process has been revolutionized by the use of Geographic Information Systems (GIS) and satellite imagery, allowing for more accurate delineation of enumeration areas and identification of hard-to-reach populations.

The actual enumeration period is typically short, often lasting just a few weeks, to minimize the effects of population movement on the count. During this time, a massive workforce of temporary enumerators is mobilized, trained, and deployed across the country. The logistical challenges of this operation are immense, particularly in large, diverse countries with remote and inaccessible areas.

Post-enumeration, the focus shifts to data processing and analysis. Modern censuses generate vast amounts of data that require sophisticated processing systems to clean, validate, and tabulate. Quality assurance measures are implemented at every stage to identify and correct errors, ensure internal consistency, and validate results against other data sources.

The demographic indicators derived from census data form the bedrock of population statistics. Perhaps the most fundamental of these is the total population count, which serves as the denominator for countless other statistics and indicators. Age and sex distribution data are equally crucial, forming the basis for population pyramids that visually represent a country's demographic structure.

Beyond these basic counts, censuses provide detailed information on fertility, mortality, and migration patterns. Fertility indicators such as the Total Fertility Rate (TFR) can be calculated, offering insights into a country's reproductive trends. Mortality data, while often supplemented by vital registration systems, can yield life expectancy estimates and infant mortality rates. Migration statistics, both internal and international, shed light on population movements and urbanization trends.

Household composition and family structure are other key areas illuminated by census data. These statistics reveal changing social norms, such as the prevalence of single-parent households or multi-generational living arrangements. Such information is invaluable for social policy formulation and service planning.

Education and literacy statistics derived from censuses provide a comprehensive picture of a nation's human capital. These indicators are crucial for educational planning and assessing progress towards universal education goals. Similarly, labor force characteristics, including employment status, occupation, and industry of work, offer insights into the economic structure of the population.

The socio-economic classification derived from census data is a powerful tool for understanding societal stratification and inequality. These classification systems vary between countries but typically incorporate factors such as education, occupation, income, and housing conditions. In India, for example, the census includes data on Scheduled Castes and Scheduled Tribes, which are constitutionally recognized groups that have historically faced social and economic disadvantages.

One of the most widely used socio-economic classification systems is the International Standard Classification of Occupations (ISCO), developed by the International Labour Organization. This system allows for international comparability of occupational data and is often adapted by countries to suit their specific contexts.

Housing and amenities data collected in censuses provide valuable information on living conditions and access to basic services. This includes data on housing type, tenure status, access to water and sanitation facilities, and availability of household assets. Such information is crucial for assessing quality of life and planning infrastructure development.

The granularity of census data allows for detailed geographical analysis, from national and regional levels down to small area statistics. This spatial dimension is particularly valuable for identifying disparities between different areas and targeting interventions accordingly. The advent of GIS has greatly enhanced the ability to visualize and analyze these spatial patterns.

While the decennial census remains the gold standard for comprehensive population data, many countries have introduced inter-censal surveys to provide more frequent updates on key indicators. These surveys, such as the American Community Survey in the United States, use sampling techniques to produce estimates of population characteristics between census years.

The confidentiality of individual census responses is a paramount concern in census methodology. Statistical agencies employ various techniques to ensure that published data cannot be used to identify specific individuals or households. This includes data aggregation, suppression of small cell counts, and the application of statistical disclosure control methods.

As we look to the future, the landscape of census-taking is evolving rapidly. Some countries are moving towards register-based censuses, which rely primarily on administrative data sources rather than traditional enumeration. This approach offers the potential for more frequent updates and reduced costs but requires highly developed administrative systems and robust data linkage capabilities.

The integration of big data sources with traditional census methods is another frontier in population statistics. Mobile phone data, satellite imagery, and social media analytics are being explored as complementary data sources that could enhance the timeliness and granularity of population estimates.

The COVID-19 pandemic has presented unprecedented challenges to census operations worldwide, forcing many countries to postpone or adapt their census plans. This crisis has accelerated the adoption of remote data collection methods and highlighted the importance of flexible, resilient statistical systems.

As we conclude our exploration of the population census, it's clear that this statistical endeavor remains as vital as ever in our data-driven world. The rich tapestry of demographic, social, and economic information it provides is irreplaceable, forming the foundation for evidence-based decision-making across all sectors of society. As we move forward, the challenge lies in adapting census methodologies to harness new technologies and data sources while maintaining the core principles of universality, individual enumeration, and data quality that have defined the census throughout its history.

In the next chapter, we will delve into the realm of vital statistics, exploring how birth and death registration systems complement census data to provide a dynamic picture of population change. We will examine the calculation of fertility and mortality rates and the construction of life tables, essential tools for demographic analysis and population projections.

Chapter 16: Vital Statistics

The study of vital statistics forms the cornerstone of demographic analysis and population health assessment. As we transition from our exploration of the population census in the previous chapter, we now delve into the realm of vital statistics, which provides a dynamic and continuous view of population changes. Vital statistics encompass the systematic collection, compilation, analysis, and dissemination of data related to vital events in human life, primarily births, deaths, marriages, and divorces.

Birth and death registration systems serve as the primary sources of vital statistics. These systems are crucial for maintaining accurate records of population dynamics and for informing public health policies. In many countries, the registration of births and deaths is a legal requirement, ensuring a comprehensive database of vital events. The process of birth registration typically involves recording details such as the date and place of birth, the child's name, and the parents' information. Similarly, death registration captures information about the deceased, including the date, place, and cause of death.

The importance of a robust birth and death registration system cannot be overstated. It provides the foundation for calculating key demographic indicators, tracking population growth, and monitoring public health trends. As demographer William Farr aptly noted in the 19th century, "The death-rate is a fact; anything beyond this is an inference." This statement underscores the fundamental role of accurate death registration in understanding population health.

In many developed countries, birth and death registration systems have been in place for centuries, evolving from church records to standardized government-managed systems. However, in developing nations, establishing comprehensive registration systems remains a challenge. The United Nations has recognized this issue and has been working towards improving civil registration and vital statistics systems worldwide through initiatives like the Global Civil Registration and Vital Statistics (CRVS) Program.

The quality and completeness of birth and death registration data significantly impact the accuracy of vital statistics. Underreporting of births and deaths, particularly in remote or underdeveloped areas, can lead to biased estimates of demographic indicators. To address this, many countries employ complementary data collection methods, such as sample registration systems or demographic surveillance sites, to validate and supplement their vital registration data.

Fertility rates, derived from birth registration data, are crucial indicators of population growth and demographic transitions. The Total Fertility Rate (TFR), which represents the average number of children a woman would have over her lifetime if current age-specific fertility rates remained constant, is widely used in population projections and policy planning. Trends in fertility rates can reveal much about a society's economic development, educational attainment, and cultural norms regarding family size.

For instance, the dramatic decline in fertility rates observed in many developed countries over the past century reflects significant societal changes. As noted by demographer Ron Lesthaeghe, "The fertility transition is not merely a response to altered socioeconomic circumstances impinging on parental aspirations and resources, but also the expression of secular and anti-authoritarian sentiments of generations socialized in an era of increasing individual autonomy in ethical, religious, and political domains."

Mortality rates, calculated from death registration data, provide valuable insights into population health and longevity. Age-specific mortality rates and cause-specific mortality rates are particularly important for identifying health priorities and evaluating the effectiveness of public health interventions. The Infant Mortality Rate (IMR), which measures the number of deaths of children under one year of age per 1,000 live births, is widely regarded as a key indicator of a country's overall health and development status.

The analysis of mortality patterns over time can reveal significant public health achievements and challenges. For example, the dramatic decline in infant mortality rates in many countries during the 20th century is often cited as one of the great public health successes. As public health historian George Rosen observed, "The conquest of infant mortality represents one of the most spectacular achievements of public health."

Life tables, constructed using age-specific mortality rates, provide a comprehensive view of mortality patterns in a population. They present the probability of surviving to each age and the life expectancy at different ages. Life tables are fundamental tools in demography, actuarial science, and public health planning. The concept of life expectancy, derived from life tables, has become a widely used measure of overall population health and development.

The evolution of life expectancy over time tells a compelling story of human progress. In many countries, life expectancy at birth has more than doubled over the past two centuries, largely due to improvements in nutrition, sanitation, medical care, and living conditions. This dramatic increase in longevity has profound implications for social structures, economic systems, and healthcare provision.

However, it's important to note that increases in life expectancy are not uniform across all populations. Significant disparities persist both between and within countries, often reflecting socioeconomic inequalities. As epidemiologist Michael Marmot has emphasized, "The poor health of the poor, the social gradient in health within countries, and the marked health inequities between countries are caused by the unequal distribution of power, income, goods, and services."

The analysis of cause-specific mortality data is crucial for understanding the burden of disease in a population and for guiding health policy and resource allocation. The shift in the leading causes of death from infectious diseases to non-communicable diseases in many countries, known as the epidemiological transition, is a key phenomenon revealed by vital statistics. This transition, first described by Abdel Omran in 1971, has significant implications for health systems and public health strategies.

In recent years, the integration of vital statistics with other data sources has opened up new avenues for demographic and epidemiological research. Linking birth and death records with other administrative data or survey data can provide rich insights into the social determinants of health and the long-term consequences of early life experiences. For instance, studies linking birth records with later life outcomes have contributed to our understanding of the fetal origins hypothesis, which posits that conditions in utero can have lifelong health effects.

The advent of digital technologies has revolutionized the collection and dissemination of vital statistics. Electronic registration systems have improved the timeliness and accuracy of data collection, while online databases have made vital statistics more accessible to researchers and policymakers. However, these technological advancements also raise important questions about data privacy and security.

As we look to the future, the importance of vital statistics in informing policy and research is likely to grow. Emerging challenges such as climate change, global migration, and population aging will require robust demographic data for effective planning and response.

Moreover, the integration of vital statistics with big data and advanced analytical techniques promises to yield new insights into population dynamics and health trends.

In conclusion, vital statistics, encompassing birth and death registration, fertility and mortality rates, and life tables, provide an essential foundation for understanding population dynamics and health trends. As we transition to the next chapter on labour and employment statistics, we will see how these vital statistics interact with economic indicators to shape our understanding of societal well-being and development. The interplay between demographic trends and labour market dynamics underscores the interconnected nature of various statistical domains in painting a comprehensive picture of a nation's socio-economic landscape.

Chapter 17: Labour and Employment Statistics

The study of labour and employment statistics forms a crucial component of understanding a nation's economic health and social well-being. As we transition from our previous discussion on vital statistics, we now delve into the intricate world of workforce dynamics, exploring the methods and metrics used to capture the pulse of a country's labour market.

Labour Force Surveys serve as the cornerstone of employment statistics, providing a comprehensive snapshot of a nation's workforce. These surveys are typically conducted on a regular basis, often quarterly or annually, to capture the ever-changing dynamics of the labour market. The methodology employed in these surveys is designed to gather detailed information about the working-age population, their employment status, and the nature of their economic activities.

One of the primary objectives of Labour Force Surveys is to determine the size and composition of the labour force. This includes not only those who are currently employed but also those who are actively seeking employment. The surveys typically use a standardized definition of employment, which allows for international comparisons. According to the International Labour Organization (ILO), employed persons are those who, during a specified brief period, performed any work for pay or profit, or had a job but were temporarily absent from it.

The process of conducting a Labour Force Survey is complex and requires careful planning and execution. Statisticians use stratified random sampling techniques to ensure that the survey sample is representative of the entire population. This involves dividing the population into subgroups or strata based on characteristics such as geographic location, age, and gender, and then selecting a random sample from each stratum. The sample size is determined based on the desired level of precision and the resources available for the survey.

Once the data is collected, it undergoes rigorous cleaning and validation processes to ensure its accuracy and reliability. Statistical techniques are applied to weight the sample data, allowing for the estimation of population parameters. This weighted data is then used to calculate various employment and unemployment indicators, which form the basis for policy decisions and economic analysis.

Employment indicators derived from Labour Force Surveys provide a multifaceted view of the labour market. The employment-to-population ratio, for instance, measures the proportion of a country's working-age population that is employed. This indicator offers insights into the economy's ability to create jobs and is often used in conjunction with GDP figures to assess economic performance. As noted by economist Joseph Stiglitz, "GDP may be going up, as measured, but increasing numbers of people are worse off. A good measure of how well we're doing is if we're able to provide jobs for everybody who wants them."

Another critical indicator is the labour force participation rate, which represents the percentage of the working-age population that is either employed or actively seeking employment. This metric is particularly useful for understanding long-term trends in workforce engagement and can reveal important societal shifts. For example, changes in female labour force participation rates often reflect evolving social norms and economic structures.

Unemployment indicators are perhaps the most closely watched statistics derived from Labour Force Surveys. The unemployment rate, which measures the proportion of the labour force that is unemployed but actively seeking work, is a key economic indicator used by policymakers, businesses, and economists to gauge the health of the labour market. However, it's important to note that the unemployment rate alone does not provide a complete picture of labour market conditions.

To address this limitation, statisticians have developed additional measures of labour underutilization. These include the underemployment rate, which captures individuals working fewer hours than they desire, and the discouraged worker rate, which accounts for those who have stopped looking for work due to perceived lack of job opportunities. As labour economist David Card points out, "Understanding the full spectrum of labour underutilization is crucial for developing effective employment policies and assessing the true state of the labour market."

Wage statistics form another vital component of labour and employment data. These statistics provide information on earnings across different industries, occupations, and demographic groups. Wage data is collected through various means, including employer surveys, tax records, and household surveys. The analysis of wage trends offers insights into issues such as income inequality, the gender pay gap, and the returns to education and skills.

One of the challenges in compiling wage statistics is capturing the full range of compensation, including non-wage benefits such as health insurance, retirement contributions, and paid leave. Moreover, the rise of the gig economy and non-standard forms of employment has complicated the measurement of wages and earnings. Statisticians are continuously refining their methodologies to address these challenges and provide a more accurate picture of workers' economic well-being.

The interpretation of labour and employment statistics requires careful consideration of various factors. For instance, seasonal variations can significantly impact employment figures, particularly in industries such as agriculture, construction, and tourism. To account for this, statisticians often produce seasonally adjusted data, which allows for more meaningful comparisons over time.

Furthermore, structural changes in the economy, such as technological advancements and globalization, can lead to shifts in employment patterns that may not be immediately apparent in aggregate statistics. As economist David Autor notes, "The nature of work is evolving rapidly, and our statistical frameworks must adapt to capture these changes effectively."

In recent years, there has been growing interest in supplementing traditional labour force surveys with alternative data sources. Big data analytics, for example, can provide real-time insights into job market trends by analyzing online job postings and professional networking sites. While these new approaches offer exciting possibilities, they also present challenges in terms of data quality, representativeness, and privacy concerns.

The COVID-19 pandemic has further underscored the importance of timely and accurate labour market statistics. The sudden and widespread disruptions to employment patterns highlighted the need for more frequent and granular data collection. Many statistical agencies responded by increasing the frequency of their surveys and developing new indicators to capture the unique aspects of the pandemic's impact on the labour market.

As we look to the future, the field of labour and employment statistics continues to evolve. There is an increasing focus on measuring the quality of jobs, not just their quantity. This includes aspects such as job security, work-life balance, and opportunities for skill development. The ILO's concept of "decent work" encapsulates this broader perspective on employment quality.

Moreover, the growing recognition of the importance of unpaid work, particularly in the care economy, is prompting statisticians to develop new methodologies for measuring and valuing these contributions. Time use surveys, which we will explore in a later chapter, play a crucial role in this effort.

In conclusion, labour and employment statistics provide a vital lens through which we can understand the functioning of our economies and societies. From the broad strokes of labour force participation rates to the nuanced details of wage distributions, these statistics inform policy decisions, guide business strategies, and shape our understanding of economic well-being. As we move forward, the challenge for statisticians will be to continue refining their methodologies to capture the evolving nature of work while maintaining the consistency and comparability that make these statistics so valuable.

As we transition to our next chapter on social indicators, we will build upon the insights gained from labour and employment statistics to explore broader measures of societal progress and well-being. The interconnections between employment, income, and various social outcomes will become increasingly apparent as we delve into indices that attempt to capture the multifaceted nature of human development and social equity.

Chapter 18: Social Indicators

The field of social indicators has grown tremendously since its inception in the 1960s, offering policymakers, researchers, and the public at large a comprehensive view of societal progress and well-being. Social indicators provide a quantitative measure of various aspects of social life, allowing for comparisons across time and between different populations. In this chapter, we delve into three crucial categories of social indicators: the Human Development Index, gender-related indicators, and poverty and inequality measures.

Human Development Index

The Human Development Index (HDI) stands as one of the most widely recognized and influential social indicators in use today. Developed by Pakistani economist Mahbub ul Haq and Indian economist Amartya Sen in 1990, the HDI was created to shift the focus of development economics from national income accounting to people-centered policies. The index encompasses three fundamental dimensions of human development: a long and healthy life, access to knowledge, and a decent standard of living.

To calculate the HDI, three sub-indices are first computed: the Health Index, Education Index, and Income Index. The Health Index is based on life expectancy at birth, reflecting the overall health and longevity of a population. The Education Index combines mean years of schooling for adults aged 25 years and older with expected years of schooling for children of school-entering age. Finally, the Income Index is calculated using the logarithm of Gross National Income per capita (PPP$), which provides a measure of the standard of living.

The HDI has been instrumental in broadening the discussion on development beyond mere economic growth. As Amartya Sen famously stated, "Human development, as an approach, is concerned with what I take to be the basic development idea: namely, advancing the richness of human life, rather than the richness of the economy in which human beings live, which is only a part of it." This perspective has led to a more nuanced understanding of development, taking into account factors such as education and health that directly impact people's lives.

However, the HDI is not without its critics. Some argue that it oversimplifies the complex nature of human development by reducing it to just three dimensions. Others point out that it fails to account for environmental sustainability or income inequality within countries. Despite these limitations, the HDI remains a powerful tool for assessing and comparing human development across nations and over time.

Gender-related Indicators

Gender equality is a fundamental human right and a necessary foundation for a peaceful, prosperous, and sustainable world. To measure progress towards gender equality, a range of gender-related indicators have been developed over the years. These indicators aim to capture various aspects of gender disparities in areas such as education, employment, political participation, and health.

One of the most comprehensive gender-related indicators is the Gender Inequality Index (GII), introduced by the United Nations Development Programme (UNDP) in 2010. The GII measures gender inequalities in three critical aspects of human development: reproductive health, empowerment, and economic status. Reproductive health is measured by maternal mortality ratio and adolescent birth rates. Empowerment is measured by the proportion of parliamentary seats occupied by females and the proportion of adult females and males aged 25 years and older with at least some secondary education. Economic status is expressed as labor market participation and measured by labor force participation rate of female and male populations aged 15 years and older.

The Gender Development Index (GDI) is another important indicator that measures gender gaps in human development achievements. It uses the same components as the HDI – health, education, and command over economic resources – but calculates these separately for males and females. The ratio of female to male HDI values provides an indication of gender gaps in human development.

In addition to these composite indices, there are numerous specific indicators that focus on particular aspects of gender equality. For instance, the Gender Parity Index (GPI) in education measures the relative access to education of males and females. It is calculated as the quotient of the number of females by the number of males enrolled at a given stage of education. A GPI of 1 indicates parity between females and males.

Another crucial indicator is the proportion of seats held by women in national parliaments. This measure reflects women's visibility in political leadership and decision-making. As former UN Secretary-General Kofi Annan once said, "There is no tool for development more effective than the empowerment of women." This sentiment underscores the importance of tracking and promoting women's participation in all spheres of life, including politics.

Gender-based violence indicators are also vital in assessing the status of women in society. These include measures such as the prevalence of intimate partner violence, female genital mutilation rates, and child marriage prevalence. While these indicators often rely on survey data and may underreport due to stigma and fear, they provide crucial insights into the challenges faced by women and girls worldwide.

It's important to note that while these indicators provide valuable information, they may not capture all aspects of gender inequality. For instance, unpaid care work, which disproportionately falls on women, is often not reflected in traditional economic indicators. Therefore, efforts are ongoing to develop more comprehensive and nuanced measures of gender equality.

Poverty and Inequality Measures

Poverty and inequality are complex, multidimensional phenomena that have far-reaching implications for individual well-being and societal progress. Measuring poverty and inequality is crucial for understanding the distribution of resources within a society, identifying vulnerable populations, and designing effective policies to address these issues.

Poverty measures typically fall into two main categories: absolute poverty measures and relative poverty measures. Absolute poverty is defined in terms of a fixed standard of living, often based on a minimum income required to meet basic needs. The most widely used absolute poverty measure is the international poverty line, currently set at $1.90 per person per day by the World Bank. This measure allows for comparisons across countries and over time, providing a global perspective on extreme poverty.

However, absolute poverty measures have limitations. As economist Angus Deaton points out, "Poverty is not just a lack of money; it is not having the capability to realize one's full potential as a human being." This insight has led to the development of multidimensional poverty measures, such as the Multidimensional Poverty Index (MPI) developed by the Oxford Poverty and Human Development Initiative and the UNDP. The MPI captures deprivations in health, education, and living standards, providing a more comprehensive picture of poverty beyond income alone.

Relative poverty measures, on the other hand, define poverty in relation to the overall distribution of income or consumption in a society. For example, the OECD often uses a relative poverty line set at 50% of the median household income. These measures capture the idea that poverty is partly about social inclusion and the ability to participate fully in society.

Inequality measures focus on the distribution of resources within a population. The most commonly used inequality measure is the Gini coefficient, which ranges from 0 (perfect equality) to 1 (perfect inequality). The Gini coefficient is based on the Lorenz curve, which plots the cumulative share of income against the cumulative share of the population. While the Gini coefficient provides a single summary statistic of inequality, it can mask important details about the distribution of income.

Other inequality measures include the Palma ratio, which is the ratio of the income share of the top 10% to that of the bottom 40%, and various percentile ratios such as the 90/10 ratio (the ratio of the 90th percentile to the 10th percentile of the income distribution). These measures can provide more intuitive and policy-relevant information about inequality at different points in the distribution.

It's crucial to note that poverty and inequality are closely interlinked but distinct concepts. As Nobel laureate Joseph Stiglitz states, "The top 1 percent have the best houses, the best educations, the best doctors, and the best lifestyles, but there is one thing that money doesn't seem to have bought: an understanding that their fate is bound up with how the other 99 percent live." This observation highlights the importance of considering both poverty and inequality in assessing societal well-being.

In recent years, there has been growing interest in measures of inclusive growth, which aim to capture how economic growth benefits different segments of the population. These measures typically combine information on both the pace and distribution of economic growth, reflecting the idea that sustainable development requires not just aggregate economic progress but also improvements in the living standards of the broader population.

The social indicators discussed in this chapter – the Human Development Index, gender-related indicators, and poverty and inequality measures – provide crucial tools for understanding societal progress and challenges. They offer policymakers, researchers, and citizens valuable insights into the multifaceted nature of human development and social well-being. However, it's important to remember that these indicators are simplifications of complex realities and should be used in conjunction with other forms of evidence and analysis.

As we move towards an increasingly data-driven world, the importance of these social indicators is likely to grow. At the same time, ongoing efforts to refine and expand these measures will be crucial to ensure they accurately reflect the evolving nature of social progress and the diverse experiences of populations around the world. The ultimate goal is not just to measure, but to use these measurements to inform policies and actions that can lead to tangible improvements in people's lives.

Chapter 19: Environmental Statistics

The field of environmental statistics has gained significant importance in recent decades as the world grapples with the challenges of climate change, resource depletion, and environmental degradation. This chapter delves into the crucial role that environmental statistics play in understanding, monitoring, and addressing these global issues. We will explore three key areas: natural resource accounting, environmental quality indicators, and sustainable development goals.

Natural resource accounting is a fundamental aspect of environmental statistics that aims to quantify and track the stocks and flows of natural resources within an economy. This approach recognizes that natural resources are finite and that their depletion can have significant economic and environmental consequences. By integrating environmental factors into national accounting systems, policymakers and researchers can gain a more comprehensive understanding of a country's true wealth and economic sustainability.

One of the primary tools used in natural resource accounting is the System of Environmental-Economic Accounting (SEEA), developed by the United Nations Statistical Commission. The SEEA provides a standardized framework for measuring the relationship between the environment and the economy. It includes accounts for natural resources such as minerals, energy, land, soil, timber, and water, as well as accounts for environmental activities and related transactions.

The implementation of natural resource accounting has revealed some startling insights into the true cost of economic growth. For instance, a study conducted by the World Bank in 2018 found that the wealth of many countries was actually declining when natural capital depletion was taken into account, despite showing positive GDP growth. This underscores the importance of looking beyond traditional economic indicators to assess a nation's long-term sustainability.

Environmental quality indicators form another crucial component of environmental statistics. These indicators provide a means of measuring and tracking various aspects of environmental health and degradation over time. They serve as essential tools for policymakers, researchers, and the public to understand the state of the environment and to assess the effectiveness of environmental policies and interventions.

One of the most widely recognized environmental quality indicators is the Air Quality Index (AQI). The AQI provides a standardized measure of air pollution levels, typically focusing on major pollutants such as particulate matter, ground-level ozone, carbon monoxide, sulfur dioxide, and nitrogen dioxide. By translating complex air quality data into a simple numerical scale, the AQI allows for easy comparison across different locations and time periods.

Water quality indicators are equally important in assessing environmental health. These may include measures of dissolved oxygen, pH levels, nutrient concentrations, and the presence of contaminants such as heavy metals or pesticides. The United Nations Environment Programme (UNEP) has developed a comprehensive set of water quality indicators as part of its Global Environment Monitoring System for freshwater (GEMS/Water) program, which helps countries monitor and report on the state of their water resources.

Biodiversity indicators are another critical aspect of environmental quality assessment. These indicators aim to measure the variety and abundance of plant and animal species within a given ecosystem or region. The Living Planet Index, developed by the World Wildlife Fund (WWF) in collaboration with the Zoological Society of London, is one such indicator that tracks global biodiversity trends. According to the 2020 Living Planet Report, there has been an average 68%

decline in monitored vertebrate species populations between 1970 and 2016, highlighting the urgent need for conservation efforts.

The development and use of environmental quality indicators face several challenges. One of the primary difficulties is the complexity of environmental systems and the interconnectedness of various factors. For example, changes in air quality can have far-reaching effects on water quality, soil health, and biodiversity. As such, developing comprehensive and meaningful indicators often requires interdisciplinary collaboration and sophisticated data analysis techniques.

Another challenge lies in the spatial and temporal variability of environmental data. Environmental conditions can vary significantly across different geographic scales and time frames, making it difficult to develop indicators that are both locally relevant and globally comparable. To address this, many environmental statisticians advocate for a multi-scale approach that combines local, regional, and global indicators to provide a more complete picture of environmental quality.

The third key area of environmental statistics we will explore is the measurement and tracking of sustainable development goals (SDGs). The SDGs, adopted by all United Nations Member States in 2015, provide a shared blueprint for peace and prosperity for people and the planet. Of the 17 SDGs, several are directly related to environmental sustainability, including clean water and sanitation (Goal 6), affordable and clean energy (Goal 7), sustainable cities and communities (Goal 11), climate action (Goal 13), life below water (Goal 14), and life on land (Goal 15).

Measuring progress towards these goals requires a robust system of environmental statistics. For example, tracking progress on Goal 13 (Climate Action) involves measuring greenhouse gas emissions, tracking the implementation of national climate change policies, and assessing the impacts of climate-related disasters. This requires the collection and analysis of vast amounts of data from various sources, including satellite observations, ground-based monitoring stations, and national inventories.

The SDGs have spurred significant advancements in environmental statistics, as countries and international organizations work to develop new indicators and improve data collection methods. For instance, the development of the System of Environmental-Economic Accounting Ecosystem Accounting (SEEA EA) framework represents a major step forward in measuring ecosystem extent and condition, as well as the flows of ecosystem services to human and economic activities.

However, significant challenges remain in measuring progress towards the SDGs, particularly in developing countries where data collection infrastructure may be limited. To address this, initiatives such as the Global Partnership for Sustainable Development Data are working to improve data availability and quality in these regions through capacity building and technology transfer.

As we move towards the conclusion of this chapter, it's important to recognize the critical role that environmental statistics play in shaping our understanding of the world around us and informing policy decisions. From natural resource accounting to environmental quality indicators and sustainable development goals, these statistical tools provide the foundation for evidence-based environmental management and sustainable development.

Looking ahead to the next chapter on "Important Surveys in India," we will explore how these global concepts and frameworks are applied in the specific context of India's statistical system. We will examine key national surveys that contribute to the country's environmental and socio-economic data, providing insights into how one of the world's largest and most diverse nations approaches the challenge of comprehensive data collection and analysis.

Chapter 20: Important Surveys in India

The National Sample Survey (NSS), Economic Census, and Time Use Survey stand as pillars of India's statistical infrastructure, providing crucial insights into the socio-economic fabric of the nation. These surveys, each with its unique methodology and focus, contribute significantly to the formulation of evidence-based policies and the understanding of India's diverse and complex society.

The National Sample Survey, often regarded as the backbone of India's statistical system, has been a cornerstone in data collection since its inception in 1950. It was established under the visionary leadership of Professor P.C. Mahalanobis, who recognized the need for a robust mechanism to gather reliable socio-economic data across the vast and varied landscape of India. The NSS operates on a continuous basis, with each round focusing on specific themes that are crucial for policy formulation and academic research.

One of the most distinctive features of the NSS is its use of scientific sampling techniques to ensure that the data collected is representative of the entire country. This approach allows for accurate estimations of various socio-economic indicators at both national and state levels, making it an invaluable tool for policymakers and researchers alike. The survey covers a wide range of topics, including household consumer expenditure, employment and unemployment, health, education, and agricultural statistics.

The household consumer expenditure surveys conducted by the NSS have been particularly influential in shaping India's economic policies. These surveys provide detailed information on the consumption patterns of households across different income groups and geographical regions. This data is crucial for understanding poverty levels, assessing the impact of various welfare schemes, and formulating targeted interventions to improve the standard of living of the population.

As noted by renowned economist Jean Drèze, "The NSS has been a goldmine of information on living conditions in India. It has played a crucial role in exposing the persistence of poverty and inequality in the country, and in guiding social policies." This statement underscores the significance of the NSS in not only providing data but also in shaping the discourse on development in India.

The employment and unemployment surveys conducted by the NSS have been equally important in understanding the dynamics of India's labor market. These surveys provide detailed information on various aspects of employment, including the nature of employment, wages, and working conditions. The data collected through these surveys has been instrumental in formulating labor policies and assessing the impact of economic reforms on employment generation.

However, it is important to note that the NSS, like any statistical endeavor, has its limitations. Critics have pointed out issues related to the timeliness of data release and the need for more frequent surveys on certain critical topics. Despite these challenges, the NSS continues to be a vital source of information for understanding India's socio-economic landscape.

Moving on to the Economic Census, this comprehensive survey provides a complete count of all establishments engaged in economic activities throughout the country. Unlike the NSS, which is based on sampling, the Economic Census is a complete enumeration exercise, covering all enterprises except those engaged in crop production and plantation.

The first Economic Census was conducted in 1977, and since then, it has been carried out at periodic intervals. The primary objective of the

Economic Census is to provide detailed information on the number of establishments, their geographical distribution, ownership patterns, employment size, and other key characteristics of the non-agricultural economy.

The Economic Census plays a crucial role in understanding the structure and composition of India's economy. It provides valuable insights into the informal sector, which constitutes a significant portion of India's economy but is often difficult to capture through conventional data collection methods. The information gathered through the Economic Census serves as a foundation for various economic policies and programs aimed at promoting entrepreneurship and small businesses.

One of the key strengths of the Economic Census is its comprehensive coverage. As stated by C. Rangarajan, former Governor of the Reserve Bank of India, "The Economic Census provides a complete picture of the entrepreneurial landscape in India. It captures the smallest of economic units, giving us a true representation of the grassroots economy." This comprehensive nature of the Economic Census makes it an invaluable tool for policymakers, researchers, and businesses alike.

The data collected through the Economic Census has been particularly useful in understanding the dynamics of India's MSME (Micro, Small, and Medium Enterprises) sector. This sector, which is often referred to as the backbone of India's economy, contributes significantly to employment generation and GDP. The Economic Census provides detailed information on the number, size, and distribution of these enterprises, helping in the formulation of targeted policies to support their growth and development.

Furthermore, the Economic Census plays a crucial role in improving the quality of other economic statistics. It provides a comprehensive frame for conducting detailed sample surveys on various aspects of the economy. The data collected through the Economic Census is used to update and improve the business registers maintained by various government agencies, ensuring that other economic surveys and statistics are based on an up-to-date and comprehensive list of economic establishments.

However, like the NSS, the Economic Census also faces certain challenges. The sheer scale of the exercise, covering millions of establishments across the country, makes it a time-consuming and resource-intensive process. Ensuring complete coverage and maintaining data quality in such a large-scale operation are ongoing challenges that the statistical system continues to address.

The Time Use Survey, the third major survey discussed in this chapter, is a relatively recent addition to India's statistical repertoire. The first nationwide Time Use Survey in India was conducted in 2019, marking a significant step forward in understanding how Indians spend their time across various activities.

Time Use Surveys are unique in their approach to data collection. Unlike conventional surveys that focus on specific aspects of socio-economic life, Time Use Surveys provide a comprehensive picture of how individuals allocate their time across various activities throughout the day. This includes not only paid work but also unpaid work, leisure activities, personal care, and other aspects of daily life.

The importance of Time Use Surveys lies in their ability to capture activities that are often overlooked in conventional economic statistics. As noted by feminist economist Devaki Jain, "Time Use Surveys are revolutionary in their potential to make visible the invisible work, particularly of women, that goes unaccounted for in traditional economic measures." This is particularly relevant in the Indian context, where a significant amount of work, especially by women, is unpaid and therefore not captured in conventional economic statistics.

The data collected through the Time Use Survey has far-reaching implications for policy formulation. It provides insights into various aspects of social and economic life, including gender disparities in time allocation, the burden of unpaid care work, patterns of leisure and recreation, and the time spent on education and skill development. This information is crucial for formulating policies aimed at promoting gender equality, improving work-life balance, and enhancing overall quality of life.

One of the key findings of India's first Time Use Survey was the significant gender gap in time spent on unpaid domestic services for household members. The survey revealed that women spent nearly 4.5 hours per day on these activities, compared to less than 1 hour for men. Such insights are invaluable for policymakers working on gender equality and women's empowerment initiatives.

The Time Use Survey also provides important insights into the informal economy and subsistence activities, which are often difficult to capture through conventional surveys. By recording all activities performed by individuals, including those that may not be considered "economic" in the traditional sense, the Time Use Survey provides a more comprehensive picture of productive activities in society.

Moreover, the Time Use Survey has significant implications for the measurement of well-being and quality of life. By providing information on how people spend their time on various activities, including leisure and personal care, it offers a more holistic view of welfare that goes beyond income-based measures.

However, it's important to note that Time Use Surveys are complex and resource-intensive. They require respondents to maintain detailed time diaries, which can be challenging, especially in a diverse country like India with varying levels of literacy. Ensuring the accuracy and reliability of the data collected is an ongoing challenge that statisticians and survey designers continue to address.

As we conclude this chapter on important surveys in India, it's clear that the National Sample Survey, Economic Census, and Time Use Survey each play a crucial role in providing a comprehensive understanding of India's socio-economic landscape. These surveys, with their unique methodologies and focus areas, complement each other to provide a holistic picture of the nation's economy and society.

The data collected through these surveys forms the bedrock of evidence-based policymaking in India. From poverty alleviation programs to economic reforms, from gender equality initiatives to labor policies, the insights provided by these surveys have been instrumental in shaping India's development trajectory.

However, in an increasingly dynamic and complex world, the challenges facing official statistics are ever-evolving. Ensuring the timeliness, accuracy, and relevance of these surveys in the face of rapid socio-economic changes is an ongoing task. The integration of new technologies, the use of big data, and the adoption of innovative survey methodologies are some of the ways in which India's statistical system is evolving to meet these challenges.

As we look towards the future, the continued refinement and expansion of these surveys will be crucial in navigating the complex challenges facing India. Whether it's addressing inequality, promoting sustainable development, or harnessing the demographic dividend, reliable and comprehensive data will remain at the heart of informed decision-making and effective governance.

www.ingramcontent.com/pod-product-compliance
Lightning Source LLC
LaVergne TN
LVHW022053200926
848481LV00003B/895
* 9 7 9 8 2 3 0 5 2 6 4 0 7 *